John Winthrop

Twayne's United States Authors Series

Pattie Cowell, Editor

Colorado State University

TUSAS 556

JOHN WINTHROP
Courtesy of the American Antiquarian Society

John Winthrop, the leader of the Puritan exodus to America, expressed his vision of the model Christian community in the New World as a "city upon a hill" to which the eyes of all the world would turn, thereby establishing a motif that has sparked the imagination of American writers for three centuries. Winthrop was the first governor of the Massachusetts Bay Colony and a central figure in shaping the character of early New England. A prolific writer, Winthrop is best known for his journal history of New England, an account that has served countless authors and historians, and for his famous shipboard sermon whose theme continues to intrigue scholars, historians, and politicians.

In this landmark study, the first to treat Winthrop's writings as a body of literature valuable in their own right and not solely for their historical or biographical significance, Lee Schweninger offers a cogent analysis of the colonist's numerous works in their political, social, theological, and literary contexts. Organized by genre and theme rather than chronologically, the study examines Winthrop's writings in light of European literary models and American influences and discusses works heretofore omitted from the available scholarship on Winthrop. The juxtaposition of lesser-known pieces with familiar works offers readers a sense of the development of Winthrop's thought and the interrelatedness of his writings. Schweninger's succinct discussions of Winthrop's life, the early days of the colony, and events like Winthrop's clash with the religious nonconformist Anne Hutchinson provide a thorough overview of the context of Winthrop's writings.

As the first book-length treatment of Winthrop's work and as an important contribution to American literary history, *John Winthrop* is certain to be welcomed by students and scholars of early American literature, history, and culture.

John Winthrop

By Lee Schweninger

University of North Carolina, Wilmington

Twayne Publishers
A Division of G. K. Hall & Co. • *Boston*

John Winthrop
Lee Schweninger

Copyright 1990 by G. K. Hall & Co.
All rights reserved.
Published by Twayne Publishers
A Division of G. K. Hall & Co.
70 Lincoln Street
Boston, Massachusetts 02111

Copyediting supervised by Barbara Sutton
Book production by Janet Z. Reynolds
Book design by Barbara Anderson

Typeset in 11 pt. Garamond
by Compset, Inc., of Beverly, Massachusetts

Printed on permanent/durable acid-free paper
and bound in the United States of America

First published 1990
10 9 8 7 6 5 4 3 2 1

Library of Congress Cataloging-in-Publication Data

Schweninger, Lee.
    John Winthrop / by Lee Schweninger.
        p.   cm. — (Twayne's United States authors series : TUSAS 556)
    Includes bibliographical references.
    ISBN 0-8057-7547-1 (alk. paper)
    1. Winthrop, John, 1588–1649.   2. Massachusetts—Governors—Biography.
3. Puritans—Massachusetts—Biography.   4. Puritans—Massachusetts—
History—17th century.   5. Massachusetts—   History—Colonial period, ca.
1600–1775.   I. Title.
F67.W79S39   1990
974.4'02'092—dc20   89-35909
                                                                            CIP

For
Everett Emerson

Contents

About the Author

Since receiving his Ph.D. from the University of North Carolina, Chapel Hill, Lee Schweninger has been assistant professor of English at the University of North Carolina, Wilmington, where he teaches primarily American literature and composition. Besides his ongoing involvement with early American literature, his research interests include romantic and later nineteenth-century literature. He has edited and introduced a collection of Puritan sermons, *Departing Glory: Eight Jeremiads by Increase Mather,* for Scholars' Facsimiles and Reprints, and has written several entries for the *Encyclopedia of American Literature* (Ungar Press). He has also published articles on Hawthorne and later nineteenth-century writers.

Preface

As first governor of Boston, John Winthrop recorded the political and social history of the Massachusetts Bay Colony from its inception in 1630 until his death in 1649. Because he stood at the center of New England politics as governor or deputy governor for virtually all of those nineteen years in New England, and because of the public-record nature of much of his writing, his later biography is, to a large extent, New England's early history. His journal history of New England is one of America's first histories, and much subsequent scholarship depends on his accounts. Winthrop's political and ethical savvy enabled the colony to survive the difficult years of its infancy; his vision of a city on a hill as a model Christian commonwealth established a motif that has sparked the American political and literary imagination for more than three centuries.

Much of what Winthrop wrote after he left England in 1630 was characterized by the perpetual battle that he saw raging between the Puritan emigrants and Satan. Winthrop made an account of the special favor he felt God was willing to show New England and the group of colonists who established their outpost in the wilderness. His record of their constant struggles against such obstacles as sickness, hunger, tempests, war, mutiny, and civil and ecclesiastical strife are, to the governor, simply manifestations of the continual efforts of Satan's armies to overthrow and ruin the chosen people's commonwealth. As his writings suggest, Winthrop believed that the colony's survival depended on the colonists' ability to thwart Satan's attempts to subvert their holy intentions.

The present study investigates the writings of the Massachusetts Bay Colony's first governor in their historical, political, social, theological, and literary contexts. The study should provide a coherent picture of Winthrop's writings, not only valuable in their own right, but also representative of his age—an age radically different from but contributing to the shape of our own. The study acknowledges Winthrop's European models and also suggests the uniquely American characteristics of his work. I attempt to establish a canon for a writer whose literary achievement has heretofore been overshadowed by his historical significance as the Bay Colony's first governor and his importance as a historian. A determination on the literary value and canonical place of his writings for the most part remains to be seen, but in an environment that continually questions the principles behind establishing literary figures and reprinting their works, the writings of John Winthrop definitely deserve reevaluation.

The first chapter briefly summarizes Winthrop's life in England and New England, suggesting some biographical reasons for the governor's having come to write what he wrote the way he wrote it. The suggestion is that recognition of the man behind the work should help in the comprehension not only of the age in which he wrote but also of the writing itself. The second chapter investigates the young Puritan's thoughts concerning his early Christian life as recorded in a diary, "Experiencia," and in a conversion narrative written when Winthrop was nearly fifty years old. The third chapter focuses on the literature Winthrop wrote or helped to write as he prepared himself, his family, and his fellow Englishmen for the migration to America; particular attention is devoted to his "Arguments for the Plantation of New England," his lay-sermon, and his "Humble Request," a document asking for the sympathy of those remaining in England. The fourth chapter investigates a troubled governor's *Short Story of the rise, reign, and ruin of the Antinomians,* a response to the Antinomian Controversy that threatened to tear the colony apart within the first decade of its existence. The next two chapters consider Winthrop's magnum opus, his journal history of the Bay Colony, from historical and literary points of view. The seventh chapter fills out the writer's literary career by discussing many of the political tracts and other works Winthrop penned as governor of Massachusetts Bay Colony. The eighth chapter speculates briefly on the contribution of Winthrop's writing to American politics, history, theology, and literature.

After nearly three and a half centuries, it is difficult to assess fairly a writer's character in the context of his own time. Although it sometimes appears simple to point out certain shortcomings from the perspective of a new age and to insist on a person's biases and mistakes, it is crucial that the student of Winthrop, as of any writer from any historical period, keep in mind the restrictions that an age imposes on the individuals living, working, and writing within it. Perhaps one of the lessons to learn from Winthrop and his writings is that the people of any age are bound by the political and religious constraints of their own era. John Winthrop was a man of his time, limited by the errors of his age, but he was also a visionary who had the strength of faith to envision, initiate, and nurture a holy commonwealth beyond the limited experience of his age. He possessed the political expertise to govern that wilderness colony through its infancy, and he had the power of intellect to articulate his vision and to record the history of that city on a hill.

For the sake of simplicity, throughout the text I refer to dates in the new style in accordance with modern practice, dating the new year starting with January rather than in the old style, starting with March. John Winthrop's new year began in March, not January, and he dated his journal and manuscripts accordingly. February was thus the twelfth month, March the first.

Although James Savage's editions (1825–26; 1853) of Winthrop's journal are the most complete, they are not as readily available as is the later James Kendall Hosmer edition (1908; reprinted in 1966). Throughout this text, therefore, I use the Hosmer edition in referring to the journal.

In quoting from the various versions of Winthrop's texts, I have tried to be as true to the original as possible. Quotations from the journal reflect the fact that Hosmer reproduced Savage's modernized spelling. In quoting documents from the unmodernized *Winthrop Papers,* I have retained original spellings, changing only certain individual letters to conform with modern typographical practice. Whereas Winthrop used *v* and *i* where modern practice prescribes *u* and *j,* for example, I have used *u* and *j* respectively.

References to primary works by Winthrop appear in the text and are identified by the following abbreviations:

DFP: A Declaration of Former Passages, 1645.
J: Winthrop's Journal: History of New England, 1630–1649, 2
    vols., 1908; reprint, 1966.
SS: A Short Story of the rise, reign, and ruin of the Antinomians,
    1644; reprinted in David D. Hall, ed., *The Antinomian*
    Controversy, 1636–1638, 1968.
WP: Winthrop Papers, 5 vols., 1929–1947.

Lee Schweninger

University of North Carolina, Wilmington

Acknowledgments

I thank the Faculty Research and Development Fund at the University of North Carolina, Wilmington, for providing travel money that enabled me to visit the library collection at the Massachusetts Historical Society in Boston. I am indebted to the staff at the Massachusetts Historical Society itself for kindly helping me use original Winthrop papers and many other related materials in the archives there. For their patience and helpfulness I thank the reference and interlibrary loan staff at Randall Library on the campus of the University of North Carolina, Wilmington. I am especially indebted to Everett Emerson at the University of North Carolina, Chapel Hill, who so willingly and helpfully read a manuscript draft of this book.

Chronology

1588   John Winthrop is born, near Groton, Suffolk, England, to Adam and Anne Browne on 22 January.

1602   Admitted to Trinity College, Cambridge, on 8 December.

1603   Begins college at Cambridge, 10 February.

1605   Leaves Cambridge; marries Mary Forth.

1607   Begins his spiritual diary, "Experiencia," on 2 February.

1609   Keeps first court at Groton Hall.

1613   Studies law at Gray's Inn in London.

1615   Mary Forth dies in June; Winthrop marries Tomasine Clopton on 6 December.

1616   Tomasine Clopton Winthrop dies in December.

1618   Winthrop marries Margaret Tyndall.

1627   Begins work at the Court of Wards and Liveries.

1629   Leaves the Court of Wards and Liveries in the early summer; spends summer and early fall writing his "Arguments for the Plantation of New England"; is elected governor of the Massachusetts Bay Company on 20 October.

1630   Sails for New England; writes the first entry of his journal history of the Bay Colony on 29 March; delivers his lay-sermon, "Modell of Christian Charity," aboard the *Arbella.*

1634   Voted out of the governorship in May elections.

1636   Writes "Christian Experiences" partly in response to the currently raging Antinomian Controversy.

1637   Reelected governor in May; begins manuscript debate with former governor, Henry Vane, concerning rights to emigration.

1640   Voted out of governorship in May.

1642   Reelected as governor.

1644   Writes small treatise on "Arbitrary Government"; Account of Antinomian Controversy, *Antinomians and Familists condemned by the synod of elders in New-England,* published in London; reprinted same year as *A Short Story of the rise, reign, and ruin of the Antinomians, Familists & libertines.* . . . Again voted out of governorship.

1645   Stands trial, having been accused by town of Hingham for overstepping authority; publishes *A Declaration of Former Passages Betwixt the English and the Narrowgansets.*

1646   Reelected to governorship and serves until his death.

1647   Margaret Tyndall Winthrop dies on 14 June.

1648   Winthrop marries Martha Rainsborough Coytmore.

1649   Winthrop dies in Boston on 26 March.

1790   First publication of Winthrop's journal, *A Journal of the Transactions and Occurrences in the Settlement.* . . .

Chapter One
The Life of a Governor

That talent, which God hathe bestowed upon him.
(Winthrop Papers, 2:133–34)

John Winthrop, the first governor of the Massachusetts Bay Colony, was born in 1588, the year Queen Elizabeth's navy defeated the Spanish Armada in the English Channel. The coincidence of his birth and this great sea battle is noteworthy because the English victory over the Spanish significantly influenced the England in which Winthrop was to grow up. In overcoming the Spanish, the English defeated what had been Europe's strongest navy and greatest military power. The victory ushered in England's superiority on the seas and guaranteed her ability to establish and hold colonies in the New World. The English themselves understood this victory as showing that God preferred England and the English to Spain and the Spanish, a preference that made manifest God's sanction of Protestantism over Catholicism. England's first major step towards becoming a world power and John Winthrop thus share the same year of birth.

Protestantism had first come to England during Henry VIII's reign in the sixteenth century, and with it came the dissolution of the Catholic monasteries. In an effort to maximize support among the merchant, professional, and noble classes, as the story goes, Henry shared the wealth of his confiscation. He needed support for his denial of the pope's authority; to gain it he offered to sell the properties of the monasteries he had dissolved. With the sale of estates to those who were already or could thereby become wealthy, landed gentry, a new and larger class of landowners came into being, and this class supported their benefactor, the king.

In 1544 Adam Winthrop (1498–1562), a London cloth merchant, bought the manor of Groton (formerly the Abbey of Bury St. Edmunds) in Suffolk, about one hundred miles north of London. The new owner's son, also named Adam Winthrop (1548–1623), inherited the manor and additional lands his father had acquired.[1] By 1600, the Winthrop head of household was a member of the elite, among the wealthiest men in England. On 22 January 1588, into this class was born John Winthrop, the only son of Anne Browne and Adam, the lord of the manor.

Winthrop biographers are fortunate because, in addition to the father's few brief diary entries concerning John's boyhood, the governor himself wrote a retrospective account of his youth in the 1630s.[2] Although little is known of his very early life, it is clear that by 1595 John was preparing for college under the tutelage of John Chaplyn. The future governor was just fifteen in 1603 when he entered Trinity College at Cambridge; in his journal for 10 February 1603, John's father Adam merely notes "my sonne went to Cambridge" (*WP*, 1:84).[3]

According to accounts of college life in the early 1600s, we can assume that at Cambridge, John, like the other young students, spent most of his morning hours reading Latin textbooks and listening to lectures in Latin; afternoons consisted of private study or attendance at public disputations.[4] Theological controversies were an important part of a college student's intellectual life, and Winthrop may well have participated in such controversies. Despite reading and working with tutors, morning lectures, and daily prayer meetings, the student had much of the day to spend on his own. The system at Cambridge certainly allowed a fifteen-year-old boy ample time to become homesick. According to his own account of the experience, he spent many hours questioning himself and his relation to God.

The young Winthrop appears to have felt himself "neglected and despised" while at Cambridge. His feelings can be attributed, in part, to the loneliness of a young student away from home for the first time. Another factor contributing to his discontent might be that the young Puritan was unpopular, indeed even disliked; after all, according to his own report, he concerned himself with such seemingly minor sins as swearing and occasionally neglecting God, while his classmates, in contrast, meanwhile amused themselves by playing dirty tricks on one another by day, and letting a woman visit them from room to room by night.[5] John himself, however, seems to have been "preserved" from such "foule sins" (*WP*, 1:155).

Winthrop seems to have been more devout and more conscious of his sins than many of his classmates. He recalls that at the age of ten, for example, he "had some notions of God, for in some great frighting or danger, [he had] prayed unto God" (*WP*, 1:154). At age twelve, he was already reading about religion and could, "under some restraint" of his natural reason, command himself. A few years later, when he was away from home at college, he again thought he had found peace with God, but later confessed that his feelings were brought on by fever and loneliness, not the true spark of grace: "I recovered my perfect health, and met with somewhat els to take pleasure in, I forgot my former acquaintance with God, and fell to former lusts, and grew worse then before" (*WP*, 1:155).

Whatever were the lusts and desires of his "voluptuous heart," Winthrop survived two years at Cambridge before he returned to Groton. According to Samuel Eliot Morison, "Few sons of the country gentry took university degrees in those days unless they were destined for the Church." It is also possible that two years of college were sufficient for preparing Adam's heir to manage the estate at Groton. Whatever the reason or reasons for his leaving Cambridge, he would not assume full responsibility for Groton until he was thirty. Before then he was to marry three times. Winthrop's biographer, Robert C. Winthrop, in fact, argues that an "early marriage . . . brought his college-life so prematurely to a close."[6]

In 1605, at age seventeen, John married twenty-one-year-old Mary Forth, sole heir of the John Forth estate. The couple's fathers had arranged the marriage, as was customary among the seventeenth-century landed gentry. Adam Winthrop makes the following note in his diary: "my soonne was sollemly contracted to Mary Foorth by Mr. Culverwell Minister of great Stambridge in Essex, *cum consentu parentum* [with consent of the parents]" (*WP*, 1:88). The only surviving description of Mary Forth Winthrop is her husband's brief statement in his diary account about talking to her concerning the life of the spirit: "it pleased God even then to so open hir hearte as that she became very readie and willinge to lay open hir hearte to me in a very comfortable measure . . . *she proved after a right godly woman*" (*WP*, 1:163).

Although there were evidently some questions about the spiritual basis of the marriage, the union undoubtedly added to the outward wealth of the Winthrop estate. Even had John not inherited Groton, he would still have been comfortably wealthy as lord of the Forth lands in Great Stambridge. Mary Forth Winthrop brought six children into the world, three boys—John, Jr. (1607–76), Henry (1608–30), and Forth (1609–30)—and three girls—of which only Mary (1612–43) survived infancy. In June of 1615 their mother, Mary, died; she was only thirty-one.[7]

Within six months of his first wife's death, John married again. Thomasine Clopton was in her early thirties and the daughter of another esquire, this one of nearby Castleins Manor. Thomasine died in the first year of their marriage, on 6 December 1616, shortly after giving birth to Winthrop's seventh child, a daughter who did not live more than two days. In his diary, "Experiencia," the bereaved husband recounts his second wife's deathbed trials and describes her as 'a woman wise, modest, lovinge, and patient of injuries; but her innocent and harmles life was of most observation. She was truly religious, and industrious therein" (*WP*, 1:190).

In April 1618, John married Margaret Tyndal. She seems to have been a wonderfully congenial match for John. As religious as he, she evidently cared much for her four stepchildren, and she bore eight children of her own, four of whom—Stephan (1619–58), Adam (1620–52), Deane (1623–1704), and Samuel (1627–74)—survived infancy. The devoted wife and mother evidently willingly decided to accompany her husband to the New World when he decided his mission was to go. Her letters show her to be articulate, loving, and wise. She epitomizes the perfect seventeenth-century Puritan wife.[8]

After Margaret's death in June 1647 and two years before his own death, Winthrop married a fourth time. His last bride was a widow, Martha Rainsborough Coytmore.

Through his first wife, Winthrop became acquainted with the Puritan minister Ezekiel Culverwell and his ministry in Essex. Here he "first found the ministry of the word to come to [his] heart with power" (*WP*, 1:155). John Winthrop thus established his Puritanism, the force behind his eventual departure for New England. The beliefs he developed in these years would determine his actions for the rest of his life. Because of the incredible force Puritanism had on everything John Winthrop did and believed, an understanding of Winthrop's religion is crucial to an understanding of the man and his works.

English Puritanism came of age, in a sense, during Queen Elizabeth's reign in the late sixteenth century. Her reign witnessed a movement toward reforming the Church of England by combining new Protestant doctrines with traditional Catholic rituals and ceremony. Before Elizabeth, as we have seen, Henry VIII (reigned 1509–47) had broken with the pope in the 1540s. During and after the reign of his son Edward VI (1547–53), writings arguing for the sole authority of scripture by such Protestant reformers as William Tyndale (1492?–1536) became influential. After a brief return to Catholicism with Queen Mary (reigned 1553–58), Protestantism returned to stay with the ascension and reign of Queen Elizabeth I (reigned 1558–1603).[9]

The term *Puritan* applied to several different groups of English Protestants during the late sixteenth century. The Puritans most closely related to the later New England colonists believed that they could best carry out God's will through membership in a purified church, one freed of the ritual and hierarchy associated with the Church of England. Yet these Puritans were willing to remain a part of the Church of England while they attempted to reform that church from within. In essence, the members of this group were practicing a type of nonconformity, which consisted of ridding the Anglican church, the Church of England, of any ritual, ceremony, or organizational structure that did not have the authority of the Bible. At the same time Puritans adopted a new moral code that defined a way of life consistent with their interpretation of the commandments and the life of Christ. They based their beliefs on the Bible as the sole true and reliable guide to belief and practice, a body of tenets verbalized by their intellectual leader, Thomas Cartwright (1535–1603). Another spokesman of Puritan practice, William Perkins (1558–1602), subscribed to Cartwright's view and developed thorough descriptions of the practical applications of his beliefs.

For Puritans who believed wholeheartedly in the Calvinist notions of predestination and the absolute power of God, a major concern was the nature of religious conversion. According to Puritan doctrine, salvation or—in Puritan terminology—justification, came about only as a result of God's predetermination. It was an Arminian heresy to assume that the Almighty could be swayed by people's efforts on earth. In other words, you cannot choose God; only God can choose you. As William Perkins explains concerning those God has chosen, "God will not judge their doings by the rigour of his law, but will accept their little and weak endeavour to do that which they can by his grace." For those chosen, God's sense of justice is satisfied by the death of Jesus on the cross; thus Christ is the sole author of a person's salvation. The elect are saved by faith, a faith made possible only by God's gift of grace. Regardless of how liberal, just, or merciful one is, without "the Spirit of Christ to create faith in the heart and sanctify him, he is as far from salvation as any other."[10] God calls a person to salvation through preachers, and the role of the Puritan preacher, according to William Perkins, is, like all else, defined by scripture. The biblical preachers Ezra and others "read in the book of the law of God distinctly, and gave the sense and caused them to understand the read-ing."[11] In short, the task of the minister was to preach in a plain style, letting the word of God speak for itself.

Several characteristics of Puritanism are important in relation to John Winthrop and the eventual Puritan migration to the New World. Though they did not want to separate from the Church of England, the group of Puritans did practice nonconformity. They insisted on eradicating from Anglican services all their Catholic ceremonial ten-dencies. They wanted to abolish the hierarchy, that is, to do away with the bishops, or any others who stood between them and God. They advocated the use of the Bible as their sole authority. In order to promote proper understanding of the Bible, Puritans supported a well-educated clergy and encouraged a literate lay population. They sub-scribed to a covenant of grace, accepting the idea that God preordained salvation and acknowledging that good works played no part in one's receiving the gift of that salvation, yet insisting on the necessity of a person's desiring justification and behaving accordingly. They put great stress on the need to examine one's heart to see if one was truly saved.

A sincere commitment to life as a Puritan in seventeenth-century England did not discourage adherents from thriving in their chosen secular professions. Indeed, Puritans often saw career success as a sign of God's favor,[12] but the successful Puritan needed to keep in mind that earthly wealth was vanity and that success came only as a result of God's will. Earthly success was not necessarily a sign of a person's own eternal worth. Thus John Winthrop, as devout a Puritan as any, stud-ied law at Grey's Inn in London for a year in 1613. While married to his first wife, Mary Forth, Winthrop also lived on his father-in-law's lands at Stambridge, probably helping to manage the estate. Sometime around 1618 John held his first court at Groton and probably shortly thereafter took over management of the ancestral manor. Although he could not have known it then, the managerial experience he gained in his years on the Forth and the Winthrop estates would prove invaluable experience for his governance of Massachusetts Bay Colony, a much larger and more complex manor.

By the early 1620s, Winthrop's work called him often to London. Working as he did among the lawyers and politicians of the city, he witnessed much immorality. His sense of propriety prompted him to write to his brother-in-law, Thomas Fones, describing "this sinful lande." Thus, as early as 1622, he expresses his dissatisfaction with a degenerate England. In 1624, in collaboration with others, he drew up a list of "Common Grevances Groaninge for Reformation," suggesting that—despite his dissatisfaction with government—Winthrop and the others were intent upon reforming, and hence remaining in, England.[13]

During the 1620s relations between the Church of England and the Puritans grew steadily worse. Charles I married a Roman Catholic woman; Bishop Laud moved to prohibit that mainstay of Puritan practice, independent preachers (preachers free of state control). For Winthrop the situation did not become critical until late in the decade. At first he went about his affairs with little encumbrance. He was politically active, working within the system, drafting bills and evidently working closely with those in Parliament. He was still firm in the belief that reformation would come from within. There is a hint of unrest when Winthrop mentions the possibility of emigrating to Ireland as his uncle (also named John Winthrop) had already done. But he seems to have had no serious thoughts of migration before 1628 and 1629 when the prospect of settling in New England presented itself. In the meantime Winthrop procured a prestigious and lucrative job as an attorney at the Court of Wards and Liveries, when he served from January 1627 to June 1629.[14] As an attorney Winthrop handled cases in which estates came into the possession of minors (wards); because minors could not control their own estates, the court dealt with cases and disputes in their management.

The actual incentive for Winthrop's emigration came late in the decade, probably as late as the spring of 1629. The attorney had to decide between London and his occupation at court or Groton and life in the country. In the city the rise of Arminianism (a doctrine differing from Winthrop's Calvinism on several points, most conspicuously the belief that good works helped one attain salvation) was in Winthrop's eyes turning the church backward and ever more toward Catholicism. Protestants in general abhorred Catholicism, but the horror was especially intense for Puritans who found even the Church of England too weighed down with ceremony, ritual, and prelacy. A political impetus for Winthrop's decision to leave England came early in 1629 when Charles I dissolved Parliament for its attempt to overrule the king's edicts.

In addition to dismaying national problems (internationally, too, Protestants were losing ground in Germany, Spain, and France), Winthrop had personal tribulations to confront. His sons were coming

of age, demanding a means of subsistence. Winthrop feared that if he
remained in England he would not have the means to support them or
himself. These problems he would mention briefly in the tract he prepared that summer describing his reasons for emigrating, "Arguments
for the Plantation of New England" (1629). He generalized about his
reasons in a letter to his wife in May: "the Lorde hath admonished,
threatened, corrected, and astonished us, yet we growe worse and
worse. . . . [H]e hath smitten all the other Churches before our
eyes. . . . I am veryly persuaded, God will bring some heavye Affliction upon this land, and that speedylye." Winthrop continues by suggesting that if "the Lord seeth it wilbe good for us, he will provide a
shelter and a hidinge place for us and ours" (*WP,* 2:91–92).

Could Winthrop have meant that hiding place to be New England?

The first step toward hiding—whether in the hinterlands of England
or in the wilderness of America—was for Winthrop to disburden himself of his job as attorney. Hence shortly after the Easter term, April
and May 1629, he could write to his wife from London, "my Office is
gone" (*WP,* 2:99). It is unknown whether he voluntarily resigned his
position or was asked to resign because of his being a Puritan, but he
certainly no longer held the post by June 1629.

If Winthrop indeed sought a hiding place, the formation of the Massachusetts Bay Company in the following months must have seemed
especially opportune. Another major step toward Winthrop's leaving
England was his making a commitment to the group of men intent
upon emigrating to New England. Essentially similar to any other
trading company of the time, this company differed in one major characteristic: its members had managed to obtain possession of the company charter or patent, and thus they could take it with them to the
New World. With possession of the patent that established their rights
and privileges, they could control their own government and elect their
own magistrates. The group elected Winthrop their governor in October 1629, and he could humbly write that "the wellfare of the plantation depends upon my assistance: for the maine pillars of it beinge
gentlemen of highe qualitye, and eminent partes, bothe for wisdome
and godlinesse, are determined to sitt still, if I deserte them." In a
later draft he makes the same point, referring to himself in the third
person: "It is com to that issue as the successe of the plantation depends
upon his [Winthrop's] goeing for the chiefe supporters (uppon whom
the rest depends) will not stirr without him" (*WP,* 2:125, 148).

Winthrop set sail for New England in the spring of 1630. His wife

Margaret remained temporarily in England, ostensibly to sell the manor at Groton, but probably her being several months pregnant discouraged her from sailing with her husband. Winthrop's eldest son, John, Jr., also remained temporarily in England to manage affairs and help sell the manor. Another son, Henry, accompanied his father to New England where he drowned shortly after their arrival.

It is difficult for the twentieth-century student of Puritan New England to comprehend the magnitude of Winthrop's decision to leave England for the virtually unknown shores of North America. In his homeland he had friends, lands, position, and wealth. He could be sure of family and friends regardless of the political and religious climate in London. But he decided to leave all this behind. His faith in Puritanism, his sense of his calling, and his dissatisfaction with the Old World prompted him, or forced him, out of the comfort, away from the sureties, of his known life. He was willing to sacrifice his comforts in the world he knew for an experimental holy commonwealth in New England. Even the sea journey itself presented the emigrant with an arduous challenge. The passengers suffered delays, the threats of pirates, storms, periodic calms, and the ever present danger of the ship's breaking down.[15] For one who had heretofore been a lifelong landlubber, even the first ten weeks of his New England experience must have tested his faith repeatedly.

Aboard the *Arbella,* the fleet's flagship, Winthrop began his journal, the manuscript that has become one of the most important documents concerning the history of the early Massachusetts Bay Colony. He also composed and evidently delivered a lay-sermon, the "Modell of Christian Charity" (1630), in which he described the kind of holy commonwealth he hoped to establish on the shores of New England, a commonwealth in which everyone would have need of the other and all would work together in a bond of brotherly affection to build a city on a hill.

In June the band of Puritan dreamers reached Massachusetts, and within a few weeks the trading company became a colony consisting of several small towns, clustered around the Charles River and the Shawmut peninsula. Winthrop first considered establishing his residence in New Towne (later Charlestown), but shortly changed his mind and settled on the Shawmut peninsula, which would become Boston, the center of New England politics, trade, and religion.

An account of the rest of Winthrop's life is also an account of the history of early America. His role as either governor, deputy governor, or assistant for all nineteen years of his life in New England (1630–49) kept him at the center of the Bay Colony's politics, church polity, and international affairs. Much of this history (his history) will consequently receive detailed attention in the context of Winthrop's writing about the colony. The events are also important as influences on Winthrop's life and literary career, however, and thus they are fittingly the subject of this chapter.

Winthrop's political career in New England is highlighted by several remarkable episodes in the history of the colony. In his attempts to establish his city on a hill he demanded conformity in belief and acceptance of the magistrates' authority. Because of the strict rules and stringent demands and because of the land's presenting the colonists with irresistible temptations, Winthrop's story is in part the tale of his periodic confrontations with degeneracy, immortality, and backsliding.

In his first few years as governor, Winthrop's task was to establish, organize, and operate a church-state system that would best provide for the immediate needs of the settlers.[16] The times were hard, and mere subsistence was certainly a high priority at the beginning of the settlement. Winthrop's journal is full of descriptions of the severity of the weather and the shortages of good food. His letters back to England during the first few years of the settlement also indicate his concern for the physical well-being of the colonists and their new colony.[17]

As soon as the settlers filled their bellies and warmed their bodies, however, contention broke out. One of the first problems concerned the magistrates' authority. The deputy governor, Thomas Dudley (father of the poet Anne Bradstreet), was evidently jealous of Winthrop's power and dominance; in 1632 he challenged the governor's authority. Because the General Court, the legislative and judiciary body for the Colony, met only quarterly, Winthrop took it upon himself to make decisions between sessions whenever an issue demanded immediate attention. He approved the building of a fishing weir, for example, before the court met because waiting would have caused the fishermen to miss the season. Winthrop defended himself by answering that "he could not be charged that he had taken advantage of his authority to oppress or wrong any man, or to benefit himself; but, for want of a public stock, had disbursed all common charges out of his own estate" (*J*, 1:87–88).[18] Even though Winthrop was able to satisfy his accusers, at least temporarily, the notion that he had overreached his authority persisted, and in the court of elections in 1634, held annually in May, the freemen voted to replace their first governor with Thomas Dudley.

Winthrop would remain very much at the center of New England politics despite his position as assistant, but for the next three years (May 1634–May 1637) he was out of the governorship and lacked the power and authority he had had. Perhaps, however, the colony missed his authority even more than he missed it himself. During his time out of office, internal strife tore at the colony and eventually even brought it to the brink of civil war. Thus Winthrop's first political defeat constituted a major early turning point for both the governor and the colony itself.

Controversy over the politics of Roger Williams brought a major test for the new administration. Williams was an outspoken, persuasive, radical separatist who maintained that the colonists were living a lie by not formally separating from the Church of England. He arrived in 1631 and immediately refused to replace Pastor Wilson at Boston's church because of its failure to make an official break with the Church of England. Williams then moved between Plymouth and Salem, preaching separatism and what Winthrop judged to be other dangerous and erroneous notions.

Williams was repeatedly called before the General Court to answer for his controversial opinions. The Court ultimately banished him in October 1635. Meanwhile, Winthrop, who could only be repelled by Williams's outspoken rebellion and by his philosophy, undoubtedly sat against him at the Court. Nevertheless Winthrop seems to have maintained an affection for the young separatist. It was Winthrop who warned him to avoid being forcibly sent back to England; and it was Winthrop with whom Williams corresponded for the next several years concerning religious matters and relations between colonists and Indians.[19]

As dangerous as Williams's threat to the colony had been, it was only child's play compared with the next major confrontation between the colony and a radical contingent. By the time Williams had been safely disposed of, Anne Hutchinson and her detachment—supported by the radical minister John Wheelwright and the young governor, Henry Vane—threatened to split New England both ideologically and politically. Even though Winthrop was able to appreciate the great mind of Roger Williams despite their differences in opinions, he could never tolerate Hutchinson despite—or perhaps because of—her intelligence and evident articulateness. This woman of "ready wit and bold spirit," as Winthrop described her, troubled the colony from 1636 until her excommunication in the spring of 1638. Thereafter, she continued to find place in Winthrop's journal until her death at the hands of the Indians in 1643.

Anne Hutchinson, as we shall see, inspired Winthrop to a most prolific outpouring of writing. He recorded the General Court's proceedings against her and eventually saw his account published, first as *Antinomians and Familists condemned by the synod of elders in New-England* (London, 1644), and later the same year as *A Short Story of the rise, reign and ruin of the Antinomians* (London, 1644), the title by which it is popularly known. His experience with the Antinomians may also have prompted his narration of the events of his own religious conversion experiences, "Christian Experiences." The controversy also moved him to write several other tracts, letters, and arguments.

Hutchinson had become a threat to the colony while Winthrop served as deputy governor. The then governor, young Henry Vane, adhered to Hutchinson's antinomianism and was obviously her highest-ranking and most influential public supporter, though the Boston minister John Cotton also supported her for a time. The division that resulted from the differences between the two factions nearly destroyed the colony.

As deputy governor, Winthrop did not have the power to discourage or thwart Hutchinson, but in May 1637 a majority of the freemen evidently felt Winthrop was the one to bring the colony back together. His reelection to the governorship after three years' absence provided the Boston establishment with the authority to suppress the religious rebels. Within a few months of his election, Winthrop had seen both Hutchinson and Wheelwright banished. Again Winthrop had overcome his opposition and established stability in the colony.

Regardless of the triumph, whether it was his election to the governorship or the expulsion of radical elements in the community, the stability Winthrop established in his commonwealth was short-lived. While the affair with Hutchinson and other matters of state consumed Winthrop's attention, he neglected his personal affairs. About 1640 he discovered that Thomas Luxford, the man he had hired to manage his land and business, had run him into great debt. That Winthrop could let his property get so out of hand and fail to keep a closer watch on his personal concerns is strong evidence of his trust in his fellow man, his innocence, and his preoccupation with governing the colony regardless of the personal costs. By the time he realized what was happening, his steward had incurred for him a monstrous debt of 2500 pounds, a debt that forced him to sell much of his land and to move to a humbler dwelling. He eventually received donations from his constituency to help him get out of debt. Winthrop lost his fortune; Luxford lost his ears.

All this while his city on a hill was dispersing both internally and externally. Such prominent men of the establishment as Thomas Hooker and John Haynes had moved to Connecticut, beyond the Bay Colony's jurisdiction. In response to this dispersal and the threat from Indians Winthrop formed a United Confederation of Colonies "for mutual help and strength" to continue as one union despite the distances between individual townships (*J,* 2:100).[20]

Another problem for Winthrop came by way of yet another radical thinker. The published attacks of Samuel Gorton in Patuxet, Rhode Island, caused Winthrop repeated consternation. The Indians, too, were a constant trial to the colonists. Having initially planned on sharing the truth of Jehovah with them, the colonists ended up fighting them for land and trade privileges. Wars or skirmishes with Indians were a constant vexation to Winthrop, prompting his tract on Indian affairs: *A Declaration of Former Passages and Proceedings Betwixt the English and the Narragansetts* (1645).

Toward the end of his political career, as in the beginning, his constituency challenged his authority. In an affair over his rightful possession of a sow, Winthrop was forced to defend his belief in the appropriateness of the magistrates' right to veto, or the right of the negative vote. Winthrop argued that without the magistrates' power to veto the deputies' decisions, those most qualified to govern would be rendered ineffectual. Like the magistrates, the deputies constituted a group of elected officials, but Winthrop saw them as representatives whose role was to inform the magistrates of public opinion. Magistrates would retain legislative authority. Because the deputies were in the majority, they would be able to carry any vote unless Winthrop took the precaution of establishing the negative voice. Without this power to veto, argued Winthrop, the Massachusetts Bay Colony would be a mere democracy, a form of government abhorred by political philosophers in the seventeenth century. The controversy inspired his writing of a tract on the subject of the negative vote.

Another battle over Winthrop's alleged abuse of authority resulted from the magistrates' attempt to reinstate their favorite rather than the people's choice as captain of the Hingham militia. In 1645 the Hingham party accused Winthrop of overstepping his authority and charged him at court. The court agreed to question him formally. He took the defendant's seat, sat uncovered as a defendant rather than as a judge or magistrate, and once again defended himself against his accusers. He argued that he accounted it "an honor put upon him, to be singled out from his brethren in the defence of a cause so just . . . and of so public concernment" (*J*, 2:233). He considered the Hingham faction mutinous and argued that he did his duty by bringing them to order.

Winthrop was cleared of any criminal charges, and as a summation of the ideology behind his actions, he presented his "little speech on liberty," arguing in essence that, once elected, magistrates have their authority from God and that the freemen and all colonists should understand liberty as the privilege "to enjoy such civil and lawful liberties, such as Christ allows" (*J*, 2:239). Winthrop's philosophy of liberty is consistent with his age, especially with the Puritan conception of authority and obedience. Moreover, this is the principle by which, as we shall see, Winthrop governed the colony and approached his political writings. The indication that the New England electorate was in agreement with Winthrop is clear. After the trial concerning the Hingham militia captain in 1645, Winthrop was reelected to the governorship each May for the rest of his life.

In 1635, sometime after Winthrop had been voted out of the governorship for the first time, Israel Stoughton wrote that Winthrop's failure to win reelection was a blessing: "He hath lost much of the applause that he hath had (for indeed he was highly magnified), and I heard some say they put in blanks not simply because they would not have him a magistrate but because they would admonish him thereby to look a little more circumspectly to himself. He is indeed a man of men, but he is but a man, and some say they have idolized him and do now confess their error."[21]

Despite Stoughton's misgivings, Winthrop was undoubtedly praiseworthy and much respected among his contemporaries. Even the subversive Thomas Morton could find nothing worse than "Temper-Well" as a disparaging epithet for the governor. Winthrop served as governor for twelve of his nineteen years in New England. He was the only governor during those years to serve consecutive terms, and besides Thomas Dudley, the only one even to be reelected. His contemporaries recognized his abilities and returned him again and again to a position of power. His strengths were evident in his ability to govern, to keep the peace when other governors could not, and to record the history of his commonwealth. His weaknesses and shortcomings were those of his age, not of his own making. John Winthrop died 26 March 1649 in the Puritan city he founded.

Winthrop's political policies and his literary output were both dependant to a great extent on his Puritan beliefs, many of which he acquired at a young age. His beliefs were of paramount importance not only to the way he lived and governed, but were also fundamental to the way he shaped and produced his body of written works. The next chapter turns to an investigation of the two early documents in which Winthrop records and formulates his Christian experiences as a young man.

Chapter Two

A Young Puritan's Christian Experiences

I could no longer dally with Religion.

(*Winthrop Papers*, 1:155)

Just before the birth of his first son, John, Jr., on 12 February 1606, John Winthrop began the diary in which he would intermittently record his spiritual experiences for the next thirty years. In that parenthood prompted Winthrop's writing, the new father anticipated such notable American Puritan writers as Anne Bradstreet and Cotton Mather who would also prepare written accounts of their spiritual experiences so that their children, in Bradstreet's words, could "gain some spiritual advantage by my experience."[1] At any rate it was extremely common for the Puritans, who were perpetually worried about their spiritual states, to keep diaries of their religious experiences.

Winthrop's spiritual diary comes to us from Robert Winthrop's *The Life and Letters of John Winthrop* (1864). As the biographer describes it, the surviving text of "Experiencia" was "an imperfect manuscript, stained and torn in many places, and quite illegible in others; many pages missing and many passages effaced, and plainly intended for no eye but his own."[2] Unfortunately, Robert C. Winthrop evidently thought fit to keep posterity from ever seeing the autograph manuscript of this diary. Only those sections he printed in his *Life and Letters* survive.[3] Robert Winthrop defends his decision to delete a section of the text by writing that "After this introduction, there follows a little catalogue of 'sinnes,' running through many days of many months, registered as in an account-current against himself, but written partly in cipher, and with so many abbreviations and secret signs as to be quite unintelligible to any eye but his own."[4] Modern scholarship must thus do without the original manuscript or even the complete text. According to the Winthrop specialist Richard Dunn, the manuscript of "'Experiencia' is now lost; Robert C. Winthrop, Jr. who had custody of the family papers, appears to have destroyed it out of respect for his ancestor's privacy."[5] The surviving account, however, is remarkable for what it shows of the young man John Winthrop before he became the stern, self-assured Puritan magistrate and governor who writes the history of New England in the 1630s and 1640s.

Although we can never know precisely why Winthrop as an individual began and kept this diary, such records of one's spiritual life were common in Elizabethan England. Like many other seventeenth-century diaries, Winthrop's provides a record of his experiences with his faith. The young Puritan records the frequent experience of his "weaknesse" and his "great desire of keeping peace and holdinge communion with God" (*WP,* 1:163).[6]

The opening lines of the diary suggest its pervasive theme of worldly vanity as precisely as if the author had the diary's future contents in mind when he began: "Worldly cares thoughe not in any grosse manner outwardly, yet seacreatly, togither with a seacret desire after pleasures and itching after libertie and unlawful delights, had brought me to waxe wearie of good duties and so to forsake my first love, whence came muche troble and danger" (*WP,* 1:161–62).[7] The frequent references to sins of the world suggest that Winthrop felt that he often forsook Christ, his first love. Throughout the manuscript—at least as Robert C. Winthrop presents it—John Winthrop reiterates his concern with his own sin of caring too much for this world. Even ten years after he begins the diary, he writes that "entertaininge the love of earthly things" breaks off his comfort in God (*WP,* 1:190–91).

When Winthrop confesses that he is subject to many sins, he evidently referred to such transgressions as impatience, caring too much for the world, sitting up late, omitting family exercise, using tobacco, and shooting game. Sins of the flesh include eating for pleasure rather than for mere sustenance. Idleness is another sin the diarist accuses himself of. He identifies his continual backsliding as his "owne rebellious wicked hearte yieldinge itselfe to the slaverye of sinne" (*WP,* 1:164). He is not always as specific as a biographer would like him to be, but in one instance he does suggest that a family quarrel brought to him "one morninge a great fitt of impatience, for matter betwixt my wife and my mother, which I pray God forgive me" (*WP,* 1:162). Even so, we cannot know how his fit of impatience manifested itself or how serious the quarrel was.

Winthrop's record of why he gave up the unlawful and sinful practice of shooting game inevitably amuses the modern reader. Because hunting "could not stande with a good conscience in my selfe," Winthrop lists several of his reasons for giving it up. First, he says, it is illegal; but it also offends many; it spoils more game that it gets; it is a waste of time; it is hard work; it is dangerous; it brings no profit; it is a financial risk; it is contemptible. For all these reasons, the hunter gave up his pastime. But he concludes by stating that "lastly for mine owne parte I have ever binne crossed in usinge it." In other words, Winthrop seems to have given up hunting because he was a poor shot. His resolution and covenant with God, therefore, is "to give over all-togither shootinge at the creeke" (WP, 1:165).

A sin of the flesh that seems to have given the future governor real trouble was gluttony. He repeatedly made resolutions to demonstrate more moderation in his diet. In 1612, for example, he writes that "Finding that the variety of meates drawes me on to eate more than standeth with my healthe, I have resolved not to eate of more than 2 dishes at any one meale, whither fish, flesh, fowle or fruite or whitt-meats [dairy]" (WP, 1:167).

Even such seemingly minor sins were of great importance to a Puritan. Using "wonderful" in the sense of "astonishing," for example, Winthrop writes that it is "wonderfull how the omission of the leaste dutie, or commission of evill, will quench grace and estrange us from the love of God." Winthrop also writes that "often sinninge bringes difficulty in repentinge" (WP, 1:162,167); in other words, frequent sinning makes breaking the bad habit all the more difficult: "the love of the worlde even in a small measure, will coole, if not kill, the life of sinceritye in Religion, and will abolishe the verye memorye of heavenly affections" (WP, 1:212).

Much of Winthrop's concern centers on everyday sins, transgressions such as overeating or being lazy. To help himself overcome these and other sins, Winthrop indulges in the standard Puritan practice of making a covenant with God: "I doe resolve first to give myselfe, my life, my witt, my helthe, my wealthe to the service of my God and Saviour, who by givinge himselfe for me, and to me, deserves what soever I am or can be, to be at his Commandement, and for his glorye" (WP, 1:168). The details of the covenant consist of his written list of resolutions and his promises to keep his end of the bargain. Winthrop is confident that God will keep the other end of the deal: "God give me grace to performe my promise and I doubt not but he will performe his" (WP, 1:163). For Winthrop, as for any regenerate Puritan, eternal life depended wholly on God's arbitrary grace. No works one performed could influence the Almighty. Nonetheless the same Puritans who espoused this Covenant of Grace abided by the commandments of God as they understood them through scripture. Winthrop continually revised his list of resolves, offering himself repeatedly to his Savior.

The death of John Forth, Winthrop's father-in-law, prompted the young Puritan to make several resolutions about humbling himself to work God's will. One of the resolutions was a promise to "live where [God] appoints me" (*WP*, 1:168). Even though he composed this particular list in May 1613, long before he could have envisioned moving to America, the statement proved prophetic. Winthrop was indeed to live where God appointed, but would not know it for several years to come. This private covenant between Winthrop and God anticipates his later articulation of the great public covenant between the settlers in New England and their God, the covenant that would bind the members of the Massachusetts Bay Colony to a strict moral code and would oblige the colonists to accept the restrictions of abiding by such a code.

The first years covered by the diary, as we have it from Robert C. Winthrop, consist of several entries concerning the future governor's transgressions and his promises to mend. In fact, the pages read like a catalogue of a typical Puritan's spiritual struggle with his flesh. As children of Adam, Christians must experience sin, but as believers in Christ, they hope for spiritual victory. The gaining of spiritual victory consists of repeatedly questioning one's spiritual state and battling the temptations of a weak, lustful flesh. Winthrop's diary is in large part the story of one man's battle. He summarizes his own purpose: "In these following Experiences there be diverse vowes, promises to God, or Resolutions and purposes of my heart, occasioned throughe the ofte experience of my weaknesse in such things, and my great desire of keeping peace and holdinge communion with God, many of which I have in tyme observed that I have great need to repent (in some of them) my unadvisednesse in making them, consideringe that they have proved snares to my Conscience, and (in others of them) my wretchednesse and sinne in not carefully observing them" (*WP*, 1:163–64).

In what might be called a set piece of Winthrop's "Experiencia" manuscript, the author includes an account of the deathbed trials of his second wife, Thomasine Clopton Winthrop. Despite the Puritans' practice of avoiding elaborate funerals and belief in death as the threshold of God's kingdom, deathbed rituals were significant to them. Their last days offered the dying time to prepare for death, to be with their families, and to review their lives. Deathbed rituals also served an im-

portant social purpose: they provided the dying person with an opportunity to give final instructions and exhortations to his family, friends,
and retainers. The dying received special respect because they had
achieved a special wisdom merely by being so close to entering the
Kingdom of God.[8]

In recording the experiences of Thomasine on her deathbed, Winthrop develops the theme that all of life serves to open his eyes to God's
mercy and to demonstrate his wife's strength. He also establishes a
doctrine of preparedness, he writes just after her death, "It is a better
and more safe estate to be prepared to die then to desire deathe" (*WP*,
1:193). As Winthrop's account shows, Thomasine was prepared to die
even though she in no way desired death. Winthrop demonstrates
Thomasine's strength by clearly making the point that even at the
deathbed of a relatively innocent and sweet woman, Satan is hard at
work, trying to win the soul of the most innocent and righteous. Although the minister accounted her innocent and in religion well
grounded, and although "the Devill could find nothing to laye to her
charge," she still had to resist temptation. When Winthrop records
Thomasine's struggles, he suggests that the temptation to turn away
from God and toward Satan is not only ever present but must be fought
off until the very moment of death. He writes that "she beganne to be
tempted, and when I came to hir she seemed to be affrighted, used
some speeches of Satans assaultinge hir, and complained of the losse of
hir first love" (*WP*, 1:185, 186).

The account of Thomasine's deathbed trials includes her exhortation
to the family, an account in which Winthrop records that his dying
wife "beganne very earnestly to call upon all that were about hir, ex-
hortinge them to serve God" (*WP*, 1:186). Winthrop describes a
procession; family members, friends, and people of the household all
visit her sickbed to receive her exhortation. To the servants she says,
"You have many good thinges in you, I have nothing to accuse you of,
be faithfull and diligent in your service." She also blesses the children
from Winthrop's first marriage. She calls for Winthrop's sister "and
exhorted hir to take heed of pride and to serve God" (*WP*, 1:187).

Winthrop describes her being prepared for death by recording the
conversation she has with her mother. "To hir mother she said that
she was the first childe that she should burye, but prayed hir that she
would not be discomforted at it; when hir mother answered that she
had no cause to be discomforted for hir, for she should goe to a better
place, and she should go to hir father, she replied that she should goe

to a better father than hir earthly father." Winthrop found that "Suche comforte had she against deathe that she stedfastly professed that if life were sett before hir she would not take it" (*WP*, 1:187, 189).

In addition to offering an account of Thomasine's exhortations and state of preparedness, Winthrop's "Experiencia" provides Thomasine with a eulogy in which he describes the model of a Puritan wife and woman. "She was a woman wise, modest, loving, and patient of injuries; but hir innocent and harmeles life was of most observation." She was humble, reverent, and careful in her "attendance of Gods ordinances." Winthrop praises her for her regard for his children and her "cariage towards myself." The one drawback or inconvenience of her goodness, he writes, was that "it made me delight too muche in hir to enjoye hir longe" (*WP*, 1:190).

Winthrop writes that through the experience of Thomasine's death he learned to humble himself, to clear his head and conscience, and to meditate on his own life. He also realized that works played no part in determining how the Lord would distribute mercy. The opening passage of his account of the death is in fact a discussion of the topic of free grace, a topic that was to give him so much trouble later in his life and in another country. For the present he wrote that God's "mercie is free, meere mercie, without any helpe of our owne worthe or will; so as for all good actions, we adde nothinge either to the deed or the doer" (*WP*, 1:182–83). This must have been a difficult concept for the bereaved man to accept. As Winthrop records it, Thomasine dies a slow and painful death despite her "innocent and harmeles" life. He writes that he hopes "God by suche checkes would teache me to goe wholly out of myselfe, and learne to depende upon him alone" (*WP*, 1:183).

The "Experiencia" diary demonstrates above all else Winthrop's struggles with his sense of living a good life. He knew all along that works played absolutely no part in God's mercy but knew also that accepting God's commandments was the only way to happiness. In the death of Thomasine he was consoled by the knowledge that God had nevertheless "caused my joye to surmount my griefe an 100 folde" (*WP*, 1:192). From this joy Winthrop gained an insight into a person's happy union with Christ. He discovered that "the usuall cause of the heavinesse and uncomfortable life of many Christians is not their religion, or the want of outward comforts . . . but because their consciences enforce them to leave somme beloved unlawfull libertie before their hearts are resolved willingly to forsake it: whereas if we could denye our own desires and be content to live by faithe in our God, the Christian life would be the only merrye and sweet life of all" (*WP,* 1:200). In this passage Winthrop sounded a theme that he would return to throughout his career. By restraining or constraining one's self to living a Christian life, Winthrop seems to say, a person actually could gain an otherwise unobtainable liberation. Winthrop would reiterate this message in his famous speech on liberty almost thirty years later, and this principle would characterize Puritan New England's conception of liberty throughout the first decades of the colony's existence.

Characteristic of Winthrop's style and of his age is his placement of great emphasis on God's providence. He fills the diary with references to events that fall out the way they do according to God's providence. An early example of such a providence in "Experiencia" is Winthrop's mention of the children's soup: "I acknowledge a speciall providence of God that my wife taking upp a measse of poridge, before the children or anybodye had eaten of it, she espied therein a greate spider." Evidently the spider was thought to be potentially fatal or at least dangerous to those who were about to eat the porridge. By discovering the spider before anyone had eaten the meal, Mary Forth Winthrop— by a "speciall providence of God"—saves the children (*WP,* 1:165).

Winthrop interprets these providences by explaining the Puritan belief that occurrences which are not in the ordinary course of nature often have strange effects. With great wisdom, according to Winthrop, God foresaw and appointed all natural events to coincide providentially. "Thus when God in justice hathe appointed that a wicked man shalbe cut off, he hath withall appointed that such a disease, suche a battail etc, or age it selfe shall concurre at the same instant for effecting of it, so that thoughe he dye of meer age, yet he dies by the force of Gods judgment" (*WP,* 1:238). The same certainly can be said for providences which seem beneficial, such as the children's surviving a pot of poisoned porridge. People live by the force of God's judgment.

Although Winthrop made no formal divisions between sections of "Experiencia," the entries do fall neatly, if somewhat arbitrarily, into four sections, each corresponding to a period in the diarist's life. The first section begins with Winthrop's first entry in January 1606 and ends just before the death of his second wife, Thomasine Clopton, in 1616. The second part consists of his account of Thomasine on her deathbed. The third picks up shortly after Thomasine's death and includes entries through February 1618, just before Winthrop's third marriage, to Margaret Tyndale. The fourth section begins, after a year's lapse, with an account of the birth of their son Stephen in March 1619 and includes the few scattered entries written between this event and the final entry in July 1629.

In the entries following the account of Thomasine's death, Winthrop concerns himself with what he considered the struggle between his earthly, vainglorious flesh and his austere spirit. In addition to commenting on the moral lessons he derives from his wife's untimely death, he recounts the vacillations of his soul between delight in things of this earth and contentment in contemplation of God's kingdom.

One of Winthrop's means of redress for his sinful ways is prayer. Yet prayer does not always seem to satisfy the sinner. In questioning the value of prayer, Winthrop sums up the almost paradoxical nature of Calvinism. Because of God's omnipotent predestination, works play no part in salvation; in other words, no amount of earnest progress can effect a man's salvation or damnation. Yet the saint will inevitably perform good works. Winthrop writes accordingly: Christ "hath taught me to trust to his free love, and not to the power of selfeworthe of my best prayers, and yet to lett mee see that true prayer, humble prayer, shall never be unregarded" (*WP*, 1:193).

As is typical for a Puritan conversion narrative, Winthrop's diary records both the highs and lows in his relations with the Holy Spirit. A typical high is recorded as ecstasy: "O my Lord, my love, how wholly delectable art thou! lett him kisse me with the kisses of his mouthe, for his love is sweeter than wine: how lovely is thy countenance! how pleasant are thy embracings!" But such ecstasy can as suddenly turn to remorse in the knowledge that man is but a prisoner of the flesh: "what am I but dust! a worm, a rebell, and thine enemie was I, wallowing in the bloud and filthe of my sinnes." In his account of Thomasine's death, Winthrop argues that although it is good to be prepared for death, one ought not to wish for it. Yet at some moments when he is especially aware of his own sins and weaknesses of the flesh, he hints at his own longing for the freedom death would bring. At one moment, for example, he asks "O when shall I be ridde of the burthen of this sinful fleshe!" (*WP*, 1:204, 214).

As the reader knows from the account of Thomasine's deathbed trials, the struggle against the temptation to sin ends only with death. Characteristically, the Puritan during life is never completely free of doubt. Indeed, doubt is paradoxically a sign of assurance, while surety is a sign of hypocrisy. Nevertheless, Winthrop argues that he felt his "faithe beginne to revive as a man out of a dreame," and that he "acknowledged the infallible truthe and certainty of Gods most pure and perfect worde" (*WP*, 1:214). Even though feelings of such certainty were only temporary, at one point Winthrop does describe the conviction of his salvation through Christ's love: "I was persuaded that neither my sinnes nor infirmities could putt me out of his favour, he havinge washed awaye the one with his owne bloud, and coveringe the other with his unchangeable love" (*WP*, 1:203).

After again renewing his covenant with God, Winthrop turns from the egocentrism of his narrative and posits an imperative: "Resist the Devill and he will flee from you" (*WP*, 1:215). The imperative is, grammatically at least, Winthrop's invitation to the reader to share the maxim. Of course, most likely Winthrop was addressing himself only in this passage, but one cannot but think that some audience might be intended, at least in the writer's mind. This entry which culminates in the imperative, concludes with a rhetorical "The Lorde be Praysed forever." This coda marks the end of the section; Winthrop would not make his next entry until a year later when he records the birth of Stephen.

Winthrop wrote the bulk of his "Experiencia" in two extended time periods. Although there are entries stretching over several years, the bulk of the diary concerns the year of Thomasine's death. After that outpouring, judging by what Robert C. Winthrop provides in his *Life and Letters,* John Winthrop wrote few additional entries. He records Stephen's birth in 1619 and Adam's birth in 1620. In 1628 he writes about accidents that threaten the lives of his sons, and in 1629 he writes that he was in danger when his horse fell under him. But these short paragraphs are all he seems to have time for as he grew busier and busier first with his duties as lord of Groton manor, then with his work for the Court of Wards and Liveries, and finally with his preparations for moving to New England. He would never again, as far as anyone knows, return to this diary of his spiritual life as such, but in 1636, in the midst of the Antinomian Controversy in New England, he would look back to record his conversion experience in a manuscript notebook. Unlike "Experiencia," which was almost certainly a private account of his own religious questionings and experiences, his "Christian Experience" was composed for circulation. Indeed, the surviving copy comes from the manuscript notebook on Henry Dunster, first president of Harvard College.[9]

In composing his "Christian Experience" on the eve of his forty-ninth birthday, Winthrop documented a conversion experience he had undergone twenty years before he wrote the narrative.[10] It is thus a testament both to his youthful conversion experience and to his conviction in middle age. Doubtless, Winthrop composed this conversion narrative at an important time in his life and in the life of the colony. He was nearly fifty years old, and almost three years had passed since he had served as governor. Certainly, he had a personal motive for reassessing his spiritual state.

Because it relies on the evolution of the Puritan church's requirement that a conversion narrative accompany the profession of faith of a candidate seeking church membership, the work could have been written as an example of such a testament. This context of Winthrop's writing shapes what would otherwise be largely a traditional, formulaic account of a Puritan's progress toward discovering his own saving faith. According to Robert C. Winthrop, the"Christian Experience" "presents a striking picture of a pious soul struggling under the doubts and despondencies which so often beset the religious temperament, and which the peculiar trials of his lot were so well calculated to aggravate."[11]

Although his "Christian Experience" records events of his youth and young manhood in England, the American setting is crucial to its composition. The developing church in New England found that by admitting only the spiritually reborn as members it could demand a narrative of the regenerate's conversion experience. The necessity of the narrative seems to have derived from the nature of the Puritans' Calvinism. According to Calvin, as the Puritans interpreted him, grace (God's arbitrary gift to the saved) was given freely by God; the individual person had no control whatsoever over receiving this grace. All depended on God's predestination. The regenerated person was strengthened through absolute dependence on God's will and arbitrary grace. During life these Calvinists could not be at all certain of their personal salvation.[12]

Because of the demands such an ideology put on its adherents, certain of Calvin's disciples outlined the process that a person might undergo on his or her way to regeneration. The process eventually became so stylized that one formulator of Puritan theology and practice, William Perkins (1558–1602), proposed a list of the ten steps in the morphology of conversion. By these steps the Calvinist could ascertain—though never with complete surety—the likelihood of his or her having grace, depending on his closely the conversion experience cor-

responded to the structure Perkins had provided. But fundamental to
Puritan belief, and therefore standing behind this process, was the insistence that in this world no one could ever be sure of his own justification. Only God could know who had been granted or who had been
denied grace.

According to Perkins, the ten steps were as follows. First, the reprobate becomes aware of the power of the ministry of the word, an
awareness that may be accompanied by some outward misfortune, such
as sickness, that tends to make one especially susceptible to the power
of the word. An understanding of good and evil follows this attendance
on the word, which in turn is followed by an awareness of one's own
sins. From these first three steps come what Perkins termed "legal
fear," a perception of one own helplessness and complete dependence
on the arbitrary mercy of God.

After these four steps, which even a hypocrite or a reprobate could
experience, came six steps leading toward the knowledge of salvation.
The potential saint was to consider the "promise of salvation" and to
experience a "will and desire to believe." This desire was followed by
the perpetual battle between thinking one has grace and doubting
whether or not one is truly saved. The combat continues off and on
until the moment of death, but it could also eventually lead to a sense
of assurance. Assurance is followed by "Evangelicall sorrow" and finally
by the grace to obey God's commandments.[13]

Given the rigidity and formulaic nature of the process of conversion
available to the Puritan, the narrative of the conversion experience, as
can be imagined, characteristically fell into a conventional pattern. As
Daniel Shea writes, "a seventeenth-century autobiographer would pro-
duce a fairly predictable variety of the genre." The typical narratives
tended toward "formalistic recitation and mechanical pattern."[14] No
matter how formulaic, however, the narration was intended to be a
truthful account of an honest personal experience. The members of the
congregation were meant to participate by interpreting the narrative
as part of their own spiritual progress.[15]

Although no necessary one-to-one correspondence exists between
Perkins's outline and Winthrop's record, Winthrop does somewhat me-
chanically describe several of the ten stages as he documents his own
conversion experiences. At about age eighteen, for example, Winthrop
seems to undergo the first stage according to Perkins's formula; he
discovers the power in the "ministry of the word." Through the minister, Ezekiel Culverwell, he finds he must finally take religion seri-

ously. As he records in his narrative: "under Mr. Culverwell his ministry . . . I first found the ministry of the word to come to my heart with power." He writes of himself that he "could no longer dally with Religion." Earlier in life he had had inklings of the law simply by his "naturall reason," but now he knows enough to accept "sweet invitations" and to distinguish between good and evil. He also becomes aware of his own sins, recounting that "the flesh would not give up her interest" (*WP,* 1:155, 156).

Along with his willingness to believe (a necessary part of the morphology of conversion according to Perkins), Winthrop experienced repeated doubts. In itself certainty was a sign of hypocrisy; doubt could be an evidence of grace. The greater and more sincere the doubt, the more likely the justification. Winthrop seemed to have sincerely doubted his own spiritual state, even to the point of fearing he lacked faith in Christ: "my greatest troubles were not the sense of Gods wrath or fear of damnation, but want of assurance of salvation, and want of strength against my corruptions; I knew that my greatest want was fayth in Christ, and faine would I have been united to Christ but I thought I was not holy enough" (*WP,* 1:158). Puritans felt doubt to be crucial throughout life, for in this world no one could truly see into the mind of God. As we have seen, Winthrop's account of Thomasine's death certainly suggests that for him doubt plays a central role in faith until the moment of death.

Recording his perpetual vacillation between a sense of holiness and helplessness, Winthrop makes such comments as "I forgot my former acquaintance with God"; "those affections were not constant but very unsettled"; "troubles came not all at once but by fits"; "my peace would fayle [fail] upon every small occasion"; "I was held long under great bondage to the Law (sinne, and humble myself); and sinne, and to humiliation again, and so day after day)"; and "the flesh would often shake off this yoke of the law" (*WP,* 1:155–58). Such misgivings about his perceived backslidings kept the author of this experience in perpetual doubt as to the state of his soul.

Arising from the periods of doubt and despair, as Perkins tells the aspiring saint, comes a sense of assurance. In Winthrop's terms, "Now could my soule close with Christ, and rest there with sweet content, so ravished with his love, as I desired nothing nor feared anything, but was filled with joy unspeakable, and glorious and with a spirit of Adoption. . . . I could now cry my father with more confidence." Despite his assurance, and again according to formula, he experiences

genuine sorrow for sin, not only his own but for the sin of others as
well. "My care was (not so much to get pardon for that was sometimes
sealed to mee while I was purposing to goe seek it, and yet sometimes
I could not obtaine it without seeking and wayteing also but) to mourn
for my ingratitude towards my God, and his free, and rich mercy"
(*WP,* 1:159, 160).

Finally, the regenerate must possess the grace to obey God's commandments. Winthrop seems to have mustered this grace regardless of
several severe battles with Satan: "But still when I have been put to it
by any suddaine danger or fearefull temptation, the good spirit of the
Lord hath not fayled to beare witnesse to me, giveing mee comfort,
and courage in the very pinch, when of my self I have been very fearefull,and dismayed" (*WP,* 1:160).

A case can be made for the conventional nature of Winthrop's
"Christian Experience." As Daniel Shea implies, it is like many
hundreds of others in its adherence to the formula laid down by Perkins
and other Puritan writers.[16] The account is also significantly different
from its fellows, however, in that one very likely occasion of the narrative is the Antinomian Controversy that raged in the Massachusetts
Bay Colony in the mid-1630s. Indeed, perhaps more important than
as a reassessment of his own spiritual state or as a formal statement
before the church, Winthrop's record of his conversion was a response
to the Antinomian Controversy that was raging in Boston as he composed the spiritual narrative.

Anne Hutchinson and her Antinomian followers held that because
God's grace was free, unconditionally presented at the beginning of
time regardless of the human input, no good works whatsoever could
help a person attain salvation or cost a person salvation already prede-
termined. In other words, the Antinomians relied not on moral law
but on the power of the Holy Spirit to govern their actions. Orthodox
New England Puritans like Winthrop feared that such a reliance would
lead to unlawfulness, licentiousness, and other transgressions. After
all, reasoned Winthrop and others, if not good works, what was to
keep the population from disrespecting and disobeying the law of the
Bible? In response to this fear, Winthrop had good reason to emphasize
his awareness of both the importance of free justification and of sanctification (good works) in his "Christian Experience." He makes a point
of having known long before of "the Doctrine of free Justification by
Christ." Significantly, Winthrop writes that "it pleased the Lord . . .
to manifest unto [him] the difference between the Covenant of grace,

and the Covenant of works." The concept of free grace is pleasing to the young John Winthrop, but the older Winthrop knows in retrospect that he "took occasion to bee more remisse in [his] spiritual watch, and so more loose in [his] conversation" (*WP*, 1:157, 158). Here he warns of the dangers of accepting the doctrine of free grace without a corresponding understanding of the importance of sanctification. After all, he implies, if a person as qualified as the conscientious and devout John Winthrop himself could become remiss in his spiritual duty, how negligent might the average person become? Winthrop's relation of his "Christian Experience" thus stands as more than a formulaic documentation of one man's discovering his own faith. It becomes a tract in anticipation of the dangers of Antinomianism.

Chapter Three
The Literature of Departure, 1629–1630

The successe of the plantation depends uppon his goeing.
(*Winthrop Papers*, 2:148)

As far as anyone knows, before the early spring of 1629, John Winthrop entertained no serious notion of settling anywhere outside England, and certainly not of migrating three thousand miles from his homeland to a barely populated wilderness, without church, town, or manor, to what Cotton Mather would later call "a squalid, horrid, American desert."[1] By the fall of the year, however, Winthrop no longer held his job at the Court of Wards and Liveries; he had been elected governor of the Massachusetts Bay Company; he had made plans to sell his estate at Groton; and he had arranged for his family's welfare until they could join him in America. Winthrop's decision to emigrate to New England was not an easy one, but once he had made it, he acted with determination and incredible alacrity.

In an exchange of letters with his wife in May, Winthrop suggested that he and his family might leave England. His first allusion to the possibility of emigration came in a letter in which he wrote that he feared "God will bringe some heavye Affliction upon this lande [England]" and that "If the Lord seeth it wilbe good for us, he will provide a shelter and a hidinge place for us and ours" (15 May 1629; *WP*, 2:91–92). Between writing this letter and another on 5 June 1629, Winthrop had made the arduous trip from London to Groton and back again. While at Groton the lord of the manor evidently discussed with his wife the possibility of emigrating to New England. In his June letter he alludes to a previous discussion in which he and Margaret have seriously considered the possibility of migrating, writing, "I am still more confirmed in that Course which I propounded to thee" (*WP*, 2:94). The "Course" he propounded may well have been to move family and fortune to New England, the "hidinge place" God would provide.

Certainly playing a large part in Winthrop's decision to leave England for New England was the creation that spring of the Massachusetts Bay Company. The new company began as a trading corporation, in many respects much like other New World companies such as those in Virginia and Plymouth. In the spring of 1628 a defunct Dorchester Company, organized in 1623 for fishing and trading, was reorganized as the New England Company. The company's governor, John Endicott, established a trading post at Naumkeag (later Salem) and asked for a royal charter to specify the company's land grant and governmental authority. Endicott's request resulted in the creation of the Massachusetts Bay Company, guaranteed by a royal charter of King Charles I. Like its predecessor, the Massachusetts Bay Company was intended to be a trading corporation. Its geographical boundaries in the New World would be those of the former New England Company, extending from three miles north of the Merrimack River to three miles south of the Charles River. On the east it would be bounded by the Atlantic and on the west by the Pacific Ocean.[2]

The company's members constituted a corporation consisting of twenty-six freemen. These twenty-six freemen would elect a governor, a deputy governor, and eighteen assistants to govern the company. Because the charter did not explicitly state that the company had to be located in England or prescribe London as the place for its quarterly meetings, all governing officials were free to reside in New England. Some historians argue that the omission was simply an oversight on the part of the framers. Winthrop himself, however, suggests that the omission was a conscious effort on the part of the undertakers. He writes that it was only with some difficulty that they got the specification of location rescinded. Whatever the reason or reasons for the omission, the government's failure to prescribe an English location as the Bay Company's legal address may be the single most important aspect of the charter. Without that special characteristic to give the members almost total freedom, Winthrop and his partners might not have agreed to initiate the undertaking.

Because the charter did not specify the place at which the members were to hold their meetings, the founders were able to assert their independence early in the company's existence and take the charter and whole government with them to New England. The decision was radical and made the Massachusetts Bay Company unique. In an agreement they drew up in Cambridge on 26 August 1629, the undertakers provided themselves with a formal statement of their insistence on taking the patent with them to Massachusetts. The legitimacy of the agreement, they stipulated, depended on the provision that "the whole governement together with the Patent for the said plantacion bee first by an order of Court legally transferred and established to remayne with us and others which shall inhabite upon the said plantacion" (*WP*, 2:152).

Because the founders designed and organized the company as a trading organization, the charter neither restricted nor dictated any laws concerning religious practices. Several of the members, however, were well-to-do Puritans who certainly planned on bringing their own form of religion across the sea with them. Although it is impossible to know the specific nature of the religion of all these emigrants, they are known generally to have been nonseparating noncomformists who wished to reform the Church of England by remaining within it. The details of church polity and its relationship with civic government do not seem to have been worked out before the Puritans departed. The details of governing and worshiping in the new colony would evolve as the colony grew.[3]

Between the time of his evident decision to emigrate (probably sometime around May 1629) and the drawing up of the "Cambridge Agreement" in late August, Winthrop wrote and rewrote his argument, or justification, for settling in New England. The purpose of the argument seems twofold. On the one hand, the written argument was to be circulated as a kind of advertisement, encouraging its readers to consider settling in New England. On the other hand, the argument served as a means for Winthrop himself to justify and clarify his own reasons for migrating. As Darrett Rutman argues, Winthrop had "to establish the rectitude for his decision in terms of his peers."[4] Winthrop also had to ensure the legitimacy of his departure from England by anticipating any objections held by the king and other officials, especially the antagonistic archbishop William Laud (1573–1645). Finally, Winthrop had to describe how the emigration was justifiable because it followed God's will for the English to settle in the New World. His argument includes reasons both for leaving England and for choosing to settle in Massachusetts.[5]

The surviving texts of what the editors call "Arguments for the Plantation of New England" are indicative of the several drafts and various versions that circulated in manuscript during the late summer and fall of 1629.[6] Winthrop seems to have begun writing about 12 August 1629 and to have completed a draft by the end of that month. He seems to have continued revising through October, when he was elected governor. A complete copy and perhaps final draft of the manuscript in John Eliot's hand suggests that the version of the "Arguments" that was circulated consisted of five sections: 1) "The Grounds of Settling a Plantation in New England," 2) "Some General Conclusions," 3) "Particular Considerations," 4) "Reasons to Be Considered," and 5) "Divers Objections."

In the first section, "The Grounds of Settling," which survives only in the Eliot version, Winthrop describes his reason for advocating the plantation in New England as appropriately religious; that is, one important motive was the "propagacion of the gospell to the Indians." The mere existence of a passage to the new lands, argues Winthrop, signals that it is God's will for Christians to spread the "Gospell to all Nations." In a plea that Winthrop might have thought could sway even the king, he compares the would-be English settlement with the Papists who under the Spanish flag were taking their "Religion and superstition" abroad (*WP,* 2:145, 146). A successful English settlement, Winthrop seems to infer, would enable England to compete with the Papists for Christian converts in the New World.

In this section, Winthrop also writes of domestic economics as a reason for emigrating: "Charitie to our neighbors impoverished by decay of Trade and lefte destitute of hope of imployment in tyme to come." The New World presents opportunities for successful farming and fishing. In a statement that echoes Elizabethan promotional tracts, Winthrop records the abundance, the "infinite varietie and store," of fish and fowl to be had in New England. Moreover, argues Winthrop, in New England cows will "growe to a farr greater bulke of body." Other possibilities for successful trade include furs, salt, vines, pitch, shipbuilding, the making of iron, hemp, flax, and "sarzaperilla" (*WP,* 2:146–47). For his account of the variety of possibilities for subsistence and commerce, Winthrop was undoubtedly indebted to Captain John Smith's *Description of New England* (1616) and other contemporary promotional tracts.

Winthrop argues that the means for effecting the exodus would be simple. Money and volunteers would be all that the Bay Company needed: money enough to acquire ships, stores, cattle, and horses; passengers enough to establish and run what was ostensibly to be a trading company. Interestingly enough for what was to become God's city on earth, Winthrop makes no mention of procuring ministers of the word of God. That would come later. Instead, he displayed his political savvy by naming carpenters, masons, smiths, coopers—tradesmen appropriate for a trading company—rather than churchmen. Procuring ministers did concern Winthrop, however, and his efforts in this regard are evident in a form letter he and the company members put together explaining that the Bay Company wanted "able and sufficient Ministers to joine with us in this worke" (27 October 1629; *WP*, 2:163).

There are few major differences between the three extant versions of the second section of the arguments for the New England plantation, *"Some generall conclusions showing that a person imployed heer in publicke service may yett be transplanted for the propagation of the Gospell in N. E."* The minor differences do explain each other in some cases, however, and help clarify Winthrop's meaning. The first of the general conclusions in the Eliot version reads that the work intended is "both lawfull and honorable." Another draft provides a helpful gloss on Winthrop's use of the term "honorable": "lawfull and hopefull of successe for the great good of the Church" (*WP*, 2:147, 132).

If Winthrop's background as a lawyer is evident in his concern about the legality of the migration, his skill as a rhetorician is evident in some of his other considerations. He argues that the undertakers must be "guifted for such a worke" and have the desire. Certainly, he wants no deported criminals. Nor does he want gentlemen looking for adventure or riches. In responding to the objection that other such New World plantations had had but ill success, Winthrop writes that "there were great and fundamentall errors in the other [plantations], which are like to be avoyded in this: for 1: their maine ende and purpose was carnall and not religious; they aimed chiefly at profitt, and not the propagating of Religion. 2: they used unfitt instrumentes, a multitude of Rude and misgoverned persons the verye scomme of the land. 3: they did not establish a right forme of Government" (*WP*, 2:117). Thus, according to Winthrop, the large percentage of idle gentlemen seeking quick and easy riches was largely responsible for early failures at Jamestown and the other Virginia colonies. Winthrop's desire for men with practical skills suggests that he had learned something about the reasons other companies failed.

More than any other type, of course, Winthrop wants saints. Because the raising or upholding of "a particular church is to be preferred" over remaining comfortable in one already established, members of the church could honorably undertake this migration (*WP*, 2:147). Winthrop argues that taking scandal off the whole church was preferable to working for the good of a particular individual church, and the job would require the best England could offer. According to him, it was scandalous to profess a goal of converting Indians, without employing "persons meete for such a worke" (*WP*, 2:133). Sending those who would be burdensome was wrong. Winthrop reiterates the importance of qualified, capable, gifted immigrants. After all, he argues by analogy, the Papists sent their best, and "in all Forraigne expeditions wee imploy our best statesmen" (*WP*, 2:148).

For the Winthrop biographer, certainly one of the most interesting sections of the "Arguments" is that concerning the *"Perticular Considerations in the case of J. W."* Here is a record of the personal reasons behind Winthrop's own decision to leave Groton Manor and his aristocratic world for the wilds of New England. Even though the honesty and sincerity of the reasons he gives are only conjectural (is a politician ever candid?), his statements do identify Winthrop's personal and particular motives for wanting to emigrate. His reasons for emigration must be considered important not only for the individual man but also as indicative of reasons many others would have had for migrating. After all, a well-established estate owner would not lightly undertake the uprooting and sacrifice such a migration demanded. That Winthrop was aware of the importance of his own decision as an inspiration to others is evident in one of his general observations for the plantation: "If such as are knowen to be godly and live in welth heare shall forsake all this to joyne themselves with this church and to runne their hazard it wilbe an example of great use boeth for the removinge of the scandall of wor[l]dly and sinister respects to give more life to the faith of godly people in their prayers for the plantation and alsoe to encourage others to joyne the more willingly in it" (*WP*, 2:112).

Winthrop agreed to join the company evidently primarily because, as he writes, the other "chiefe supporters (uppon whom the rest depends) will not stirr without him" (*WP*, 2:148). Winthrop's statement raises interesting questions about his importance to the company. Can this be true? Did the whole success of the plantation depend on this new member of the company? Why, for example, did the other freemen elect him governor? He was new to the company and in New England they already had a governor in John Endicott. Moreover, the election was held in the fall instead of the spring as the charter dictated. Darrett Rutman maintains that Winthrop's newness along with the consequent lack of rivalry helped him to the governorship. Stanley Gray suggests the same when, in another context, he writes that in "Winthrop's lack of novelty lies his importance."[7]

In September 1629, the company consisted primarily of three

groups, the old Dorchester group from the west of England, the Londoners, and the country gentlemen. Even though Winthrop had ties with both the Londoners and those from the country, he was "nevertheless unassociated in prior company affairs with any particular group."[8] Perhaps, then, in the early going when obtaining money and volunteers were of utmost importance, the freemen thought of Winthrop as a neutral peacekeeper, and therefore they found him extremely desirable as a governor. The other candidates' close associations with one group or another might have disqualified them as legitimate, neutral choices.

At any rate, shortly after his election, Winthrop could write in an early draft of his particular considerations that "It is come to that issue, as, in all probabilitye, the wellfare of the plantation depends upon my assistance: for the maine pillers of it . . . are determined to sitt still, if I deserte them." In another version of the same section, writing of himself in the third person, as we have seen, Winthrop reiterates his importance: "It is com to that issuè as the successe of the plantation depends uppon his goeing for the chiefe supporters . . . will not stirr without him" (*WP*, 2:125, 148).

If this statement seems arrogant, certainly the next is humble and candid enough. He states that he cannot afford to remain in England. He has three sons coming of age and simply cannot meet the expenses of the life that his position as lord of a manor demands. At one point in the "Arguments," for example, he exclaims that "noe mans estate allmost will suffice to keepe saile with his equalls" (*WP*, 2:139).[9] Another apparent incentive for his emigration is the fact that his wife and children support him in his decision and are voluntarily willing to go. A private motive becomes public in a later draft: as a Puritan he feels it his duty to seek the conversion of the heathen and thereby to compete with the Papists in gaining converts. Primarily, however, Winthrop wishes to spend the remainder of his time on earth in the best service of his church. He feels he can best serve God and his church by utilizing his talent as a public servant doing public service. Evidently, Winthrop feels his election as governor signals his life's calling: "I have a lawfull callinge, outwarde, from the Chiefe of the plantation, approved by godly and judicious divines: and inwarde by the inclination of mine owne heart to the worke" (*WP*, 2:126).

In an autograph draft of the "Reasons to Be Considered" for the plantation, Winthrop lists several reasons for migrating to New England. Settling in New England would serve the church in different ways. By carrying the gospel to new parts of the world, the Puritans would avoid the ever-present danger of corruption from the desolate churches of Europe. Another reason for migration was that England "growes weary of her Inhabitantes" (*WP,* 2:139). Winthrop argued humanely, that whereas human beings were considered vile and burdensome in England, in New England they would be precious and necessary, as human beings should be in God's world. The whole earth is the Lord's, declares Winthrop, and should be settled by godly men.

As a nonconforming member of the Church of England, Winthrop walked a narrow line between a desire to reform the church from within and an urge to abandon the Anglican church altogether and become a Puritan radical or Separatist. As if aware of his ticklish situation, he omits mentioning England when he verbalizes another ground for departure as the "Danger and extremities of the present estate of the Churches both in forraigne parts etc." (*WP,* 1:147). Does he intentionally omit naming England as a place where the church is in danger? Perhaps he did not need to mention the Church of England because its problems were self-evident, or perhaps he shunned the danger of offending readers who did not feel that the church in England was as corrupt as foreign churches. It is impossible to know whether Winthrop failed to elaborate on the location of the churches that were in such a dangerous state, but from other sources it is known that he feared the corrupt state of the churches in England. In a letter to his wife Margaret, for example, he writes that the Lord "hath smitten all the other Churches before our eyes, and hath made them to drinke of the bitter cuppe of tribulation . . . [and now] is turning the cuppe towards us also, and because we are the last, our portion must be, to drinke the verye dreggs which remaine: my deare wife, I am verily perswaded, God will bringe some heavye Affliction upon this lande, and that speedilye" (*WP,* 2:91).

Winthrop also argues that the godly and well-to-do people's giving up the comforts of England would both encourage others of similar social stature and make evident the holy and worthwhile nature of the migration. In this context, Winthrop mentions a reason that he used elsewhere to suggest that God sanctioned the endeavor. If many godly people take it up, it must have the Lord's sanction: "It appeares to be a worke of God for the good of his Church in that he hath disposed the hartes of soe many of his wise and faithfull servantes both ministers, and others not onely to approve of the enterprise but to interest themselves in it" (*WP,* 2:140).

Throughout his "Arguments for the Plantation of New England," Winthrop incorporates biblical passages as a necessary part of his discourse. Here as elsewhere in his writing he makes frequent reference to the history presented in the scriptures to note parallels between the New England venture and similar historical endeavors. As was typical of Puritan writers relying on scripture for historical precedent, he rarely referred to nonbiblical or pagan examples.

In the final section Winthrop answers some of the *"Divers objections which have been made against this plantation."* One objection that concerned Winthrop repeatedly was the Puritan's taking the land from the native Americans. He demonstrated the ethnocentrism of his times by writing that because the Indians "inclose noe Land, neither have any setled habitation, nor any tame cattle to improve the Land by" they had no real need of that land. Besides, he adds, if the English leave the Indians enough land for their own use, the settlers "may lawfully take the rest." Further, argues Winthrop, the plague that had left so few Indian survivors was a sign that the English had God's approval (*WP*, 2:141). And if all this was not enough, the English had the surviving Indians' permission to settle in New England.[10]

Another consideration that troubled Winthrop was whether it was noble or godly to forsake England in the country's time of need. Was it not perhaps God's will that he and his Puritan brethren remain in England to fight the battle for a reformed church on English soil? In August 1629, in fact, Winthrop's friend Robert Ryece attempted to dissuade Winthrop from emigrating by arguing that the "church and common welthe heere at home hathe more neede of your beste abyllytie in these dangerous tymes, then any remote plantation" (*WP*, 2:105). Winthrop paraphrases this objection as "a great wrong to our Church and Countrie to take awaye the good people" and answers it by arguing that by going they set an example for others to turn from their evil ways, that the percentage of those going is tiny, and that "the Gospell should be preached to all nations" (*WP*, 2:141–42).

Winthrop's contemporaries who read the arguments for plantation and who signed the "Agreement at Cambridge" in the late summer of 1629 committed themselves to be ready "to embarke for the said plantation by the first of March next" (*WP*, 2:152). Between the signing and the sailing, Winthrop was busy procuring the necessities for the voyage and settlement. Letters and other documents from these months indicate his activity in obtaining ships, bidding adieu to friends, choosing ministers, securing bread and meat, convincing others to emigrate, selling Groton, and arranging for the payment of the colonists' passage.

In December 1629, as a recently elected governor, Winthrop addressed the company, asking them to turn the joint stock of the company over to ten undertakers. Winthrop writes that the "maine businesse hathe been about disengaginge and orderinge the joint stock" (*WP*, 2:175). The company favored Winthrop's request with a show of hands. Since there is no record of the repayment of the initial investment nor any direct trade profits divided at the end of the seven-year term, it is likely that what transpired at this December meeting turned out to be more important symbolically than economically. Symbolically the decision to allow the undertakers to hold the stock signified that the Massachusetts Bay Company was to enjoy an economical independence in addition to the geographical freedom guaranteed by the Charter and reiterated in the "Cambridge Agreement." None of the earlier or other existing companies had experienced such autonomy.

In addition to stating the "maine businesse" of this meeting, Winthrop used this address to reiterate or anticipate several of the themes concerning his conception of the establishment and governing of the colony. He asserts his belief, for example, that the Puritans are in some way, either in England or New England, to serve as a model and example for the rest of the world: "Consider your reputation, the eyes of all the godly are upon you, what can you do more honorable for this Citye, and the Gospell which you profess." As we shall see, this theme recurs in his shipboard sermon. Winthrop also insists that although he hopes the company would agree to divide the joint stock, no separation is intended. He requests that the members of the company "still [always] be one" (*WP*, 2:176, 175). Winthrop stressed and repeated the theme of unity, or body of one, throughout his arguments for New England.

The governor and the others who were wholly committed to the New England enterprise looked for sincere commitment from each individual undertaker. Winthrop hopes of himself, the undertakers, and worthy gentlemen in London that "we might be knit togither in a most firm bond of love and frindshippe, that you may knowe that we need your helpe and desire it" (*WP*, 2:176). The company had agreed to the necessity of a strict interdependence among members two months earlier when the framers of that "Cambridge Agreement" stipulated that "this whole adventure growes upon the joint confidence we have in each others fidelity and resolution herein, so as no man of us would

have adventured it without assurance of the rest" (*WP*, 2:152). Without this mutual commitment the company would flounder. Indeed
Winthrop's insistence on communally mutual interdependence would
follow him to the New World and remain an important theme
throughout his career as governor and historian.

Having made all necessary arrangements, Winthrop and his company were ready to sail by March. The new governor rode to Southampton on 10 March 1630, writing to his wife that "from thence I
shall take my last farewell of thee till we meet in new E[ngland]" (*WP*,
2:218). By the end of March 1630, Winthrop was at Cowes aboard a
350-ton ship awaiting departure. Within a few days settlers making
up the Massachusetts Bay Company would set sail for the coast of
North America. John Winthrop, among other passengers, would never
see England again.

While aboard the *Arbella* still in the harbor at Cowes, Winthrop and
his fellow freemen wrote and signed a short document entitled "The
Humble Request of His Majesties loyal subjects, the Governour and
the Company late gone for *New England*; to the rest of their Brethren
in and of the Church of England" (*WP*, 2:231). Although historians of
early America are undecided about the authorship of the "Humble Request," it is probably safe to assume that Winthrop played an important part in its composition. Certainly he read it, signed it, and echoed
it in his later writing.

The address is primarily a written statement by the emigrants, insisting that those men, women, and children aboard the ships were
leaving England and the Church of England out of love, not hate or
bitterness. They insist on their position as nonconforming nonsepara-
tists. The body of their company "esteeme it our honour, to call the
Church of *England,* from whence we rise, our dear Mother." The signers
of the "Request" were leaving not "loathing that milk wherewith we
were nourished there, but blessing God for the parentage and educa-
tion" (*WP*, 2:232).

Behind "such an assertion," writes Perry Miller, "it is not difficult
to trace the familiar casuistry of Non-separation."[11] Indeed, the address
must have been, at least to some extent, a final attempt on the part of
the company's members to insist on their desire to remain within the
Church of England. Regardless of his contribution to the actual composition of the "Request," Winthrop had no scruples about endorsing
the statement it made. After all, in it he essentially asks his readers,

"the ministers of God" remaining in England, not to fail to pray for the small band of dreamers about to cross the Atlantic.

In making their request, the governor and his otherwise wealthy, aristocratic associates humbled themselves before those who remained secure and comfortable in England: "We beseech you therefore by the mercies of the *Lord Jesus* to consider us as your Brethren, standing in very great need of your helpe, and earnestly imploring it." That Winthrop felt perfectly comfortable with this request is evidenced by his writing that it "is an usuall and laudable exercise of your charity to commend to the prayers of your Congregations the necessities and straights of your private neighbors." He defines the new relationship by identifying his body of emigrants as "a weake colony from your selves" and by reminding his readers with a vivid and delightful image that the emigrants were to reside in "poore cottages in the wilderness" (*WP,* 2:232–33).

In this "Humble Request" Winthrop thus places himself and his colony at the mercy of the company's brethren "in and of the *Church* of England" (*WP,* 2:231). In this particular context, he sees himself as poor and in subjection. He has given up his position of wealth and influence in England, and although the governor and his assistants hold power over the multitude aboard the ships as elected officials charged with carrying out the word of God in the wilderness, Winthrop is nonetheless humble enough to recognize, at least politically, his dependence on those who remain behind. According to the terminology of the lay sermon Winthrop would write and deliver at sea, those "eminent in power and dignity" were the elders and brethren ashore, and those "meane and in subjection" were the migrating Puritans, poor, weak, and dependent in their humble wilderness cottages (*WP,* 2:282).

As the flagship, the *Arbella,* led the fleet of eleven ships away from the southwest coast of England and ventured onto the open sea, Winthrop must have had his purpose, his sacrifice, and the precariousness of the enterprise in mind.[12] The "Humble Request" to those remaining to remember the group at sea, the list of reasons and arguments written and rewritten, the optimism of John Cotton's farewell sermon, "God's Promise to his Plantations," and his own convictions, all must have been buzzing in the governor's mind as he headed westward. Out of these thoughts grew what one historian has called Winthrop's "single most important statement," the "Modell of Christian Charity."[13]

No contemporary account mentions Winthrop actually delivering this lay-sermon; it is certainly tempting, however, to conjecture a scene in which the Puritan leader as the new civil governor stands on the deck before the assortment of passengers, and not exactly preaches, but talks in a strain that harmonizes with the open sea and the wind as he tells the story of what the commonwealth is to become. Winthrop's immediate purpose is to express the need for the whole group, rich and poor, to work together in building a Christian commonwealth in the American wilderness: "Wee ought to account our selves knit together by this bond of love, and live in the exercise of it" (*WP*, 2:292).

Winthrop's argument in the "Modell" is that God created separate classes in the human population to show glory in differences; to have more occasion to manifest the work of the spirit; and to demonstrate that "every man might have need of other" in justice and mercy. To show that mercy, Winthrop refers to the Golden Rule, warning that people should harken to Matthew: "Whatsoever ye would that men should doe to you" (*WP*, 2:283, 284). Because true mercy includes giving and practicing charity among God's children, Winthrop outlines the rules for giving and lending. What initially appears to be a statement supporting the aristocracy and perpetuating the rigid English class system can be seen conversely as an indication that Winthrop was willing to circumvent the conventional class structure insofar as the success of the plantation depends on all men and women working together, rich and poor alike.

The affection from which charity arises is love: "Love is the bond of perfection." Given this definition, Winthrop concludes that true Christians are of one body in Christ and that love is the ligament of this body. The governor elaborates this metaphor as a metaphysical poet would his conceit, explaining that all parts of the body must work together; if one member suffers, the whole suffers. Thus, all must treat their neighbors as part of themselves. As a company of true Christians on a pilgrimage to establish a Christian commonwealth, the passengers on the ships on the Atlantic are knit together as one body, each part helping the other and thereby helping itself: "wee must be willing to abridge our selves of our superfluities, for the supply of others necessities" (*WP*, 2:288, 294).

Winthrop knew the method behind the structuring of a Puritan sermon. Although his text does not actually come from the Bible, as a minister's would,[14] his initial statement does function as a kind of scriptural text: "God Almighty in his most holy and wise providence hath soe disposed of the Condition of mankinde, as in all times some must be rich some poore, some highe and eminent in power and dignitie; others meane and in subjection" (*WP,* 2:282). The orator here could easily be alluding to a passage in Deuteronomy, a passage he does actually refer to in the course of his sermon: "Because there shalbe ever some poore in the land, therefore I commande thee, saying, thou shalt open thine hand onto thy brother, to thy nedie, and to thy poore in thy lande" (Deut. 15:11).[15] In any case, as is typical in a Puritan sermon, the prophet (in this case John Winthrop) explains the context of the text. Here Winthrop elaborates on the reasons for God's so disposing "of the Condition of mankind" (*WP,* 2:282).

In what seems to parallel the typical *doctrine* section of the conventional Puritan sermon, Winthrop establishes his principles based on the "truth" expressed in the text. He purposes to develop a theory of mercy and charity by requiring that all people help one another out of the same affection that "makes him carefull of his owne good" (*WP,* 2:284). Mercy is exercised, he writes, in giving, lending, and forgiving; the affection which prompts that mercy must be love.

Winthrop refers to Colossians in defending this love: "Love is the bond of perfection," or according to the Geneva Bible, the "bond of Perfectnesse." In describing the governor as a Christian statesman, George Mosse argues that Winthrop applies Ramean logic to argue his point that all God's children are bound together by love. This system of logic derived its name from Peter Ramus (1515–72), an influential French Protestant. Winthrop stresses the essence of the principle, the cause—in this case, love—then enumerates its effects. Love is the necessary ligament of the body; no body is perfect without perfect ligaments; when one ligament suffers, the whole body suffers.[16] Winthrop refers to scripture (Col. 3:14) to define love as "the bond of perfection. First, it is a bond, or ligament. 2ly, it makes the worke perfect. There is noe body but consistes of partes and that which knitts these partes together gives the body its perfection, because it makes eache parte soe contiguous to other as thereby they doe mutually participate with eache other" (*WP,* 2:288).

To begin the third section of the lay-sermon—conventionally the *application* or *uses* section in which the speaker applies the doctrine to the particular Puritan audience—Winthrop writes that it "rests now to make some application of this discourse." He itemizes the component parts of the present endeavor: persons, work, ends, and means. The persons undertaking the establishment of his city on a hill constitute his audience, a group of professed members of Christ, "knit together by this bond of love." The work at hand is "by a mutual consent . . . to seeke out a place of Cohabitation and Consorteshipp under a due forme of goverment both civill and ecclesiastical" (*WP,* 2:292, 293). The means consist of doing the Lord's work through strict conformity and dutiful practice, two virtues Winthrop would stress throughout his literary career.

Even though conventional in its structure, the "Modell of Christian Charity" is certainly idealistic and in some ways even radical in its message. Winthrop was idealistic in his hope that despite what he considered God's division of humanity into classes, the people who were to found the colony in Massachusetts would be able to care for one another even though they had not necessarily been able to do so in England. The radical nature of the lay-sermon is evident in Winthrop's assertion that all these people, both rich and poor, educated and uneducated, godly and ungodly, would not only understand their special covenant with God, but would be willing and able to work out that covenant together. In his insistence that men give up self for the whole, Winthrop echoes John Cotton who—in his farewell sermon preached at the departure of the *Arbella*—had insisted that every man must go forth "with a publick spirit, looking not on your owne things onely."[17]

In his own sermon Winthrop describes a special covenant between the colonists and God, insisting that God has given a special commission: "Thus stands the cause between God and us, wee are entered into Covenant with him for this worke." In other words, Winthrop perceives an agreement between the colonists and God; if the colonists observe the commandments, God will bless them. "Now if the Lord shall please to heare us, and bring us in peace to the place wee desire, then hath hee ratified this Covenant and sealed our commission, [and] will expect a strickt performance of the Articles contained in it" (*WP,* 1:294). This statement anticipates the covenant theology that was to spring up in New England. Certainly it well expresses Winthrop's own understanding of the covenant he considered himself obliged to uphold.

In his "Modell of Christian Charity" Winthrop essentially transforms the company that began as a prosaic trading corporation into the epitome of the perfect church-state on earth. In his famous reference to Matthew (5:14), Winthrop acknowledges the symbolic importance of the mission those on the *Arbella* and the other ships have undertaken: "Wee must Consider that wee shall be as a Citty upon a Hill, the eyes of all people are uppon us." Even though he could boast that the world would watch the Puritans' progress, Winthrop realized that the higher the call (and these settlers certainly had a high call), the greater the risk of a devastating fall: "if wee shall deale falsely with our god in this worke wee have undertaken and soe cause him to withdrawe his present help from us, wee shall be made a story and a by-word through the world . . ." (*WP,* 1:295).

The notion of a city on a hill suggests the double meaning of the sermon's title, "Modell of Christian Charity." In one sense the "model" is simply a summary or an argument for the plantation in New England. But in another sense a "model" is an object of imitation, an exemplar. Winthrop could well have intended both meanings to work at once. His sermon provides a summary of the work the people need to accomplish, and at the same time it suggests and presents the image and outline of an ideal holy commonwealth.

Like most Puritan writers, Winthrop followed the practice of the plain style. He cited numerous biblical references in supporting his arguments and used only an occasional metaphor or other figure of speech. Most notable is the extended metaphor (echoing Eph. 4:16) associating the people of Christ as members of one body and love as ligaments holding them (it) together. As seems appropriate for a writer describing the invisible, perhaps incomprehensible, workings of God, Winthrop often uses similes to clarify his meaning. Arguing that one cannot force the affection from which mercy must arise, for example, he refers to a clock repairman mending the wheel in order to get the clock to strike (*WP,* 2:288). His analogy is that one's love must come from the soul just as the clock's work comes from a mainspring; analogously, that is, showing charity (or love) toward another is only a manifestation of the well-ordered Christian life, not an independent movement. One knows that if the mainspring works properly the clock will strike.

In a conceit that rivals those of his contemporary metaphysical poets, Winthrop describes the pleasure of love "as wee may see in the natural body, the mouth is at all the paines to receive and mince the foode which serves for the nourishment of all the other partes of the body, yet it hath noe cause to complaine," for the body sends back nourishment and the mouth receives pleasure in chewing "as farre exceedes the paines it takes" (*WP,* 2:291–92).

Besides the importance of its immediate impact and its clarification of the governor's ideals, the sermon Winthrop preached on the *Arbella* anticipates several characteristics of American literature and culture. Most obviously, perhaps, the sermon insists on the notion of America as God's country, America as the New Israel.[18] Winthrop's lay-sermon also announces the possibility of divine retribution when a chosen people backslides, a theme that will recur through American literary history. As Sacvan Bercovitch argues, the sermon can be considered emblematic of the rhetoric of mission that permeates American literature.[19]

Perhaps most significantly, the sermon demonstrates Winthrop's willingness to accept his social and economic inferiors in some sense as his equals. As we have seen, Winthrop begins his sermon with the statement that social inequality is God's decree. Winthrop's argument, however, is that despite—or because of—this decree, all have need of one another. Although he would have abhorred the thought, Winthrop planted the seed of democracy when he spoke of the "common good of the Creature" (*WP*, 2:283). We must wonder why Winthrop did not foresee that if all were considered equal in a holy commonwealth, they might go on to consider themselves politically and socially equal as well.

Composed before Winthrop ever set eyes on his New England, before the city on a hill even existed, the "Modell of Christian Charity"— conceived, written, and delivered at sea—is one of American literature's earliest important documents. In this lay-sermon that stands near the head of American literature, Winthrop anticipates many of the themes of American literature and the concept of the American dream. America is the place sanctioned by God for a chosen people. By working together, this chosen people will achieve God's will. Here, then, is the manifesto of an early dreamer of the golden dream.

Chapter Four

In Response to the Antinomian Controversy

One Mistris *Hutchinson* . . . a woman of a haughty and fierce carriage, of a nimble witt and active spirit, and a very voluble tongue, more bold then a man, though in understanding and judgement, inferiour to many women.

(Short Story, 262–63)

One of the greatest tests of John Winthrop's theory of a holy commonwealth knit together as one body came with the controversy over Anne Hutchinson and her right to differ with the authorities and to express those differences to the public. For this reason, of all the episodes of Winthrop's career, the Antinomian Controversy that raged in New England between 1636 and 1638 has received the most critical and historical attention. Critics, biographers, and historians are inevitably intrigued and troubled by the episode. Liberals judge Anne Hutchinson to be the governor's intellectual superior, and recognize a failure of justice in her banishment and excommunication. Edmund Morgan writes, for example, that "the force of her intelligence and character penetrate the libels and leave us angry with the writers and not with their intended victim."[1] Conservatives condemn Hutchinson as a contentious and proud troublemaker, a disrupter of the New Canaan.[2] In the drama of the controversy, Winthrop's part is overshadowed by the colorful and outspoken Anne Hutchinson, yet his published record of the trial of Hutchinson and his related journal entries provide the most important literary/historical sources for the controversy between the partiarchal, authoritarian church-state and Anne Hutchinson.

Daughter of the freethinking, somewhat radical schoolteacher and preacher Francis Marbury, Anne Hutchinson was born in rural Alford, England, one hundred miles due north of London, in 1591. Alford was her home until she was fourteen, at which time her father moved the family to London. In 1612 Anne married William Hutchinson, a wealthy Alford merchant, with whom she returned to Alford to bear and raise several children. She made special trips to St. Botolph's Church in Boston, Lincolnshire, where John Cotton lectured before he left for the Massachusetts Bay Colony. She evidently became spiritually enamored of Cotton's preaching and theology, and by 1634 she and her family had decided to move to the Bay Colony; they arrived in September of that year.

What finally prompted the family to give up their financial and social comforts in England and decide to settle in a new struggling colony remains a matter of speculation, but certainly the political, religious, and economic concerns of so many migrating Puritans in the 1630s played an important role in the Hutchinson family's decision to move to America.[3] According to Anne Hutchinson's testimony before the General Court in Massachusetts as Winthrop recorded it, however, she insisted that she came to New England in pursuit of her preacher and mentor, John Cotton: "The Lord carrying Mr. *Cotton* to *New England* (at which I was much troubled) it was revealed to me, that I must go thither also (*SS,* 272).[4]

Anne Hutchinson's troubles with the church in New England began with her arrival in Boston Harbor in September 1634 on the *Griffin.* Her husband, William, was admitted at once into the Church at Boston; Anne's admission, however, was initially denied. Normally, husband and wife were admitted together, but in this case the authorities delayed the wife's admittance for a week because of certain comments she had been overheard to make before setting foot on New England soil. One of her shipmates, Reverend Zachariah Symmes, evidently reported his uneasiness with her beliefs and kept her from joining the church until she could show a group of elders that her theology was sound.[5]

Despite a troublesome beginning, once established in New England Anne Hutchinson found herself immediately useful not only as homemaker for her own family, but as community midwife and healer as well; she was one of a few who knew how to mix herbs for medicinal purposes. She also found herself within a few months hosting weekly discussions pertaining to John Cotton's sermons, first with groups of women, then with mixed groups of men and women. The ostensible purpose of the meetings was to give members of the community the opportunity to discuss the meaning of Cotton's lectures. The meetings soon grew beyond mere recitations, however, and became the vehicle for the rise of what Winthrop called "Antinomianism." Hutchinson's group was by no means small or uninfluencial. Anne Hutchinson enjoyed the support of the young, newly elected governor, Henry Vane, and of the popular minister John Wheelwright, her brother-in-law. She and her supporters essentially divided Boston. In Winthrop's eyes that division threatened to disrupt the equilibrium and well-being of the entire colony.

By the time Winthrop makes his first journal entry concerning Hutchinson (21 October 1636), she had been in Boston just over two years and had become the leader of an active movement. As we can picture it, John Winthrop sat down at his desk not too long after beginning the second volume of his manuscript journal and wrote his first entry concerning Anne Hutchinson. He had known, or at least known of, Hutchinson since her arrival in September 1634. Indeed, she and her family built their house and settled literally across the street from the Winthrops. The governor begins his entry with characteristic understatement, but does carefully itemize the polity behind the dispute: "One Mrs. Hutchinson, a member of the church of Boston, a woman of ready wit and bold spirit, brought over with her two dangerous errors: 1. That the person of the Holy Ghost dwells in a justified person. 2. That no sanctification can help to evidence to us our justification.—From these two grew many branches; as, 1. Our union with the Holy Ghost, so as a Christian remains dead to every spiritual action, and hath no gifts nor graces, other than such as are in hypocrites, nor any other sanctification but the Holy Ghost himself" (*J*, 1:195–96). Winthrop's entry touches on crucial questions concerning the colonists' understanding of regeneration.[6]

Winthrop's literary outpouring in response to the Antinomian Controversy begins with this journal entry, but the governor's official account of the trials of Hutchinson and her disciples was published in London in 1644, several years after the controversy and trials of 1637 and 1638. Within the same year it was republished as *A Short Story of the rise, reign, and ruine of the Antinomians, Familists and Libertines, that Infected the Churches of New England* (London, 1644).

The original title of Winthrop's version of the Hutchinson episode indicates the thrust of his account: *Antinomians and Familists Condemned by the Synod of Elders in New-England: With the Proceedings of the Magistrates against Them, and Their Apology for the Same* (London, 1644). Winthrop loads the title with pejorative terms, each of which effectively deprecates his adversaries. Etymologically, *antinomian* means "outside or against the name or law." Used by Winthrop, the term connotes those who stood opposed to the legalism of the Bible.

Understanding the intricacies of the Antinomian controversy depends on an acquaintance with several terms bandied about by the members of the religious community. *Legalism,* as Winthrop applied the concept, referred to strict conformity to the moral codes or law of the Bible. *Justification* was a term used to connote salvation or grace (in other words, a justified person was a visible saint, one preordained by God to grace). Antinomians maintained that because justification was free—that is, because it came as a gift of God that no one could otherwise acquire—ministers should not stress the performing of good works. Rather they should emphasize free justification, also referred to as the "Covenant of grace" as opposed to the "Covenant of works." Indeed, the Antinomians accused the orthodox ministers of preaching a doctrine of works rather than a doctrine of grace. Winthrop applied the term *sanctification* or preparation to this notion of growing or earning divine grace as a result of commitment to the biblical law or moral code. According to Winthrop, as an orthodox Calvinist, of course, man did not earn justification, but could prepare to receive grace. Winthrop saw sanctification as a necessary or concomitant part of a visible saint's life in preparation to receive grace. If saved or "of the elect," one would necessarily behave as a saint. The two notions, justification and sanctification in this sense, were in some ways so interdependent as to be indistinguishable.

To a large extent, the point of contention between the Antinomians and the orthodox New England Puritans rests on the distinction between free justification and sanctification (or grace and works). As evident in his conception of New England's covenant with God, Winthrop held that a person could not be justified and not show signs of sanctification; Anne Hutchinson is reputed to have held that because justification is free, sanctification is of no concern in the eyes of God. Antinomians, including Hutchinson, relied on the power of the Holy Spirit, rather than on a moral code, to govern actions.

Winthrop thus addresses those who believed that if justification were free then sanctification (that is, behaving oneself according to biblical law and rule) had nothing, absolutely nothing, to do with one's being saved. The obvious danger of such a belief, reasons Winthrop, is that because of man's corrupt nature, it will inevitably lead to widespread immorality, licentiousness, and unnameable sins.

As Winthrop used the term in the 1630s, *familist* was a general term referring to those who relied on their own spiritual experience to interpret the Bible; that is, they believed in a direct communication between the individual and God. Like an Antinomian, a familist did not necessarily feel bound to the legalism of the Bible. The Massachusetts Bay officials feared that any such sect threatened their whole community, which was inextricably bound to upholding conduct based on the scriptural word. Because the Familists had a bad reputation in England, Winthrop gained an advantage over his opponents by associating Antinomians with Familists. Similarly, a *Libertine,* originally one who opposed the rigors of Calvinism, came to be associated with all kinds of religious freethinkers. Certainly an establishment based on conformity and dutiful practice—as was Winthrop's—did not admire or encourage freethinking in this sense.

The *Short Story* consists of several documents, some obviously not written by the governor. In addition to a long preface supplied by the Reverend Thomas Weld (who was in New England from 1632 until 1641), the collection includes a list of "erroneous opinions"; the petition that John Wheelwright's adherents devised; and Winthrop's narrative of the court cases against Wheelwright, his adherents, and Anne Hutchinson. The collection also includes Winthrop's description of Mary Dyer's "monstrous birth"; the justification of Wheelwright's censure, and a summary of Hutchinson's excommunication trial before the church. In addition to the *Short Story,* much of the history of the Antinomian Controversy can be gleaned from Winthrop's journal account of his response to the Hutchinson episode.

Winthrop had strong misgivings about the theology of Anne Hutchinson, but in 1636, as deputy governor, he could not effectively oppose her actions or reduce her influence. When she and her followers attempted to invite their colleague John Wheelwright to become an assistant teacher (that is, to accept ministerial duties) at the First Church and thereby officially establish within the system a cleric sympathetic to their views, however, the former governor became assertive. As he describes the confrontation in his journal, he "stood up and said, he could not consent." After all, he argued, the First Church already had two able ministers in John Wilson and John Cotton. Furthermore, the congregation did not know Wheelwright sufficiently well, and should not run the risk of inviting a disputatious teacher. Winthrop "thought it not fit (no necessity urging) to put the welfare of the church to the least hazard, as he feared they should do, by calling in one, whose spirit they knew not, and one who seemed to dissent in judgment." So Wheelwright was denied a position in Boston; instead, he was offered a position at a "new church, to be gathered at Mount Woolaston, now

Braintree," ten miles south of Boston along a difficult road (*J*, 1:197). In other words, Winthrop had essentially disposed of Wheelwright as a threat to the community and had won a small skirmish. But the battles ahead promised to be more difficult.

In January 1637, John Cotton seems to have invited Wheelwright to speak to the congregation at the Boston church. His sermon occasioned further dissension among the churches of Massachusetts Bay and ultimately resulted in Wheelwright's banishment. In this fast-day sermon—delivered on January 1637, a day set aside to repent for dissensions in the New England churches—Wheelwright's doctrine is that "the only cause of the fasting of true beleevers is the absence of Christ".[7] (Public fast days were common in New England as a means of repentance for the entire population. Such days did not necessarily involve total abstinence.) To Winthrop and others of the establishment even the hint of Christ's absence must have seemed an affront. Did this man (Wheelwright) not scruple to say that Christ was absent from New England, the New Canaan, God's chosen land? The notion of God being displeased and departing from New England would eventually become a popular motif for the New England ministers, but in the 1630s this idea was unwelcome and certainly offended the leaders in the congregation.

What Winthrop and others actually took Wheelwright to task for was not his references to God's departure, however. Rather Wheelwright got in trouble because of his repeated use of the metaphor of combat. In the text he admits that he intends "spirituall combate," but goes on at some length about warfare, fighting, and battle. Specifically, he argues that "if we would have the Lord Jesus Christ to be aboundantly present with us, we must all of us prepare for battell and come out against the enimyes of the Lord, and if we do not strive, those under a covenant of works will prevaile."[8] Wheelwright also seems to advocate "combustion in the Church and common wealth. . . . I must confesse and acknowledge it will do so, but what then? did not Christ come to send fire upon the earth"? He also argues that those who fight for Christ "must be willing to lay downe [their] lives."[9]

Whether Wheelwright actually intended a literal battle must remain conjectural, but his rhetoric was powerful enough to frighten the establishment. As a result of his fiery sermon, the court banished Wheelwright, and the following November he left the jurisdiction of the colony. Winthrop and the others of the established authority had thus won another political battle. Nevertheless, the sermon epitomized the division among the members of the Boston congregation and made manifest the frail hold the establishment had on maintaining conformity and keeping a peaceful unity among colonists in the Puritan commonwealth.

Another major victory for the establishment was to come by way of the May elections. At the gathering for the election a group of Bostonians in support of Henry Vane demanded that before the election a petition relating to liberty and revoking Wheelwright's banishment be heard. As Winthrop records it, "There was great danger of tumult that day." As deputy governor, Winthrop insisted that the business of a court for election is restricted to the elections themselves: "So soon as the court was set . . . a petition was preferred by those of Boston. The present governor [Vane] would have read it, but the deputy governor [Winthrop] said it was out of order. It was a court for elections." After some debate, and evidently some fistfights, elections were held; Winthrop once again became governor and Henry Vane, as Winthrop notes glibly in his journal, was "left quite out" (*J*, 1:215).

As governor (reelected in May 1637), Winthrop had the authority he had earlier lacked to deal with the Antinomians. He took immediate steps to set the colony back on its feet, writing in his journal that the "Magistrates set forth an apology to justify the sentence of the court against Mr. Wheelwright." In what is a sure sign of Winthrop's leniency and political savvy, the court granted Wheelwright a period until the following August (1637) to reform his error. Winthrop thereby hoped that the court's "moderation and desire for reconciliation might appear to all" (*J*, 1:216, 218).

Included in Winthrop's *Short Story* is the justification of the court's censure of Wheelwright. In it Winthrop summarizes the steps the court took and explains the court's reasons for those actions. The purpose was to clear the justice of the court and to satisfy those "to whom this case may be otherwise presented by fame or misreport." The court's opinion was that Wheelwright "had run into sedition and contempt of the Civill authority." (*SS*, 290, 289). The establishment ministers felt that they had been described as ones who advocated a covenant of works. As is characteristic of Winthrop's reporting, his account of the proceedings is detailed. He lists several reasons to demonstrate that the court was justified in banishing Wheelwright. Some of these reasons are that he knew he was inciting contention and that he went against Cotton's injunction about peace on a fast day. Uncharacteristically, Winthrop turns to classical authors such as Tully, Isidore, and Vergil (a turn which might suggest that Winthrop was not sole author of this tract) to define sedition, but he also refers to scripture to corroborate this definition. Returning to Wheelwright, Winthrop writes that "hee did intend to trouble our peace, and hee hath effected it; therefore it was a contempt of that authority which required every man to study Peace and Truth, and therefore it was a seditious contempt, in that hee stirred up others, to join in the disturbance of that peace, which he was bound by solemn oath to preserve" (*SS*, 294).

Because Winthrop governed and wrote in an age before the notion of freedom of speech was established, certainly before it was considered an inalienable right, he could simply respond to the objection that the court could not tell a minister what to preach by answering that it is the court's prerogative to "limit him what he may not teach" (*SS*, 295). Specifically, the court could forbid his preaching heresy or sedition. In response to the objection concerning the lack of a trial by jury, Winthrop answered according to his philosophy of the magistrates' authority: the court makes its law, is subject to no others, and has as its sole guiding principle truth and justice. A typical Puritan, Winthrop believed that a good ruler was virtually incorruptible; after all, magistrates received their authority from God and so governed by divine right. In Winthrop's mind there would be no question of the court not acting in a fair manner because it had the welfare of the state and church as its sole motive.[10]

In concluding his account of Wheelwright's banishment, Winthrop returned to his definition of sedition. Wheelwright did tend to the "great hinderance of public utility" and was therefore guilty of sedition (*SS*, 299). Such a judicial procedure might be difficult for a twentieth-century reader to accept without realizing that Winthrop was writing in the 1630s, an age when the Bill of Rights and free speech were still more than 150 years in the future. Judged in light of his contemporaries, Winthrop was in fact lenient in that he was more than willing to give Wheelwright the opportunity to reform and thereafter remain within the colony's jurisdiction. Nevertheless, in a community where all were to be bound together in one body, each limb and part helping the other, Winthrop could not allow the holding and spreading of doctrine so contrary to that of the establishment.

In September 1637 the ministers organized a synod in which they drew up the list of errors to be attributed to the Antinomians. In his preface to Winthrop's "Short Story," Thomas Weld offers a description of the synod: *"we had an Assembly of all the Ministers and learned men in*

the whole Countrey, which held for three weeks together, at Cambridge . . .
*the magistrates sitting present all that time, as hearers, and speakers also when
they saw fit."* The populace at large was also given liberty to attend and
participate as long as they observed "due order." As Weld describes the
synod, the members spent one week confuting *"loose opinions"* and two
weeks *"in a plaine Syllogisticall dispute"* (*SS,* 212, 213).

The result or product of the synod was the drawing up of eighty-
two, numbered, erroneous opinions with a confutation of each one. As
should be expected, the refutation comes from scripture; in almost
every case the erroneous opinion was found to be contrary to Scripture,
and Scripture was used to point out the error. If, for example, the error
concerned the belief that "those that bee in Christ are not under the
Law, and commands of the word, as the rule of life," the confutation
would read that it "is contrary to the Scriptures, which direct us to the
Law and to the Testimony" (*SS,* 220). The list is part of the *Short Story*
and is, of course, not of Winthrop's sole authorship (although he most
likely had a hand in establishing the various errors). According to
Philip Gura, the errors can be arranged into three major classes. One
class pertains specifically to one of the most immediate questions facing
the rulers of the Bay Colony, questions about the Antinomian controversy itself: "beliefs in the primacy of the Spirit over the injunctions of
Scripture." The second concerns the ability of a justified person to
know the condition of another. The third class covers that group of
opinions that challenge the authority of the ministers.[11]

The synod met during September 1637; in November of that year
the court brought Anne Hutchinson to trial. Winthrop and his fellow
magistrates had already dealt with many of her group, banishing
Wheelwright and dealing harshly with others. Her other most powerful ally, Henry Vane, had left the colony to return to England. Thus
she stood alone on a November morning before the court, ready to face
her accusers.

Winthrop's characterization of Hutchinson is fascinating both for its
vigor and for what it tells us about the author and his times. The others
disfranchised, banished, or disabled "were but young branches, sprung
out of an old root"; that root was Mistress Hutchinson, "a woman of
haughty and fierce carriage, of a nimble wit and active spirit, and a
very voluble tongue, more bold then any man, though in understanding and judgment, inferiour to many women" (*SS,* 262–63). The description informs us of Winthrop's animosity toward her; it also
suggests that he was subject to the sexism and biases of his time.

Hutchinson's understanding of the fine differences of theological opinion was obviously acute, and if Winthrop is referring to them he is
simply dissembling. In her understanding and judgment of a woman's
role and proper place in seventeenth-century Puritan New England,
certainly she was not deficient, but of that role she was undoubtedly
defiant.

Winthrop adds that she "had learned her skil in *England*" (*SS*, 263).
It is politically important for the governor of New England to intimate
that her erroneous opinions did not, in fact could not, originate in the
New Canaan. Rather, he suggests that she brought them with her,
already hatched and nurtured in the corruption of old England. As
proof he cites the opinions she expressed on the ship before even setting
foot in New England. Alertly he adds that the Boston church was
hesitant to admit her. To justify the church's ultimate admission of
her, Winthrop explains that "shee cunningly dissembled and coloured
her opinions." Further, she "easily insinuated her selfe into the affections of many." Winthrop's own insinuation is that much like a serpent
she slid subtly through the Boston garden. Certainly the governor was
aware of the seventeenth-century connotation of *insinuate* as "to introduce by subtle means," implying the agent's subversion and infection.
Through the tone and diction Winthrop further reprobates his adversary. Although he gives her credit for helping with the "publick min-
istery," he turns it to his own advantage: "But when she had thus
prepared the way by such wholesome truths, then she begins to set
forth her own stuffe" (*SS*, 263). Winthrop does not mince words here;
in seventeenth-century English, *stuff* commonly referred to a worthless
idea or nonsense. Winthrop's diction is clearly pejorative in his opening
description of the woman and her ideas.

In the course of his characterization of Hutchinson, Winthrop jus-
tifies his complaint by citing her teachings. Theologically the difference between her and the establishment lay in her insistence that "no
sanctification was any evidence of a good estate, except their justification were first cleared up to them by the immediate wittnesse of the
Spirit." According to Winthrop, the negative consequence of this opinion is twofold. First, she was subverting the authority of the colony,
church, and state. Second, she was inciting others: "many prophane
persons became of her opinion, for it was a very easie and acceptable
way to heaven." Winthrop feared that her opinions would become
manifest in the people's backsliding. Formerly godly people would fall

under her persuasion, and "indeed most of her new tenents tended toward slothfulnesse" (*SS*, 263, 264).

The primary charges against Hutchinson were that she taught against the ministers of the commonwealth and that she argued for the primacy of the spirit over the Scripture. Winthrop also attributed to Hutchinson "the utter subversion both of Churches and civill state." At the December 1636 session of the General Court, the Pastor John Wilson made "a very sad speech on the condition of our churches" (*J*, 1:204). This "free and faithfull speech in the Court," as Winthrop called it, caused Wilson much consternation. He was called to answer publicly. Winthrop blames Hutchinson for occasioning the speech and for causing Wilson's embarrassment: "Thence sprang all that trouble to the Pastour of *Boston*." In addition to causing problems for Wilson and the magistrates, Hutchinson received the blame for corrupting John Wheelwright, who before her influence "was wont to teach in a plaine and gentle style" (*SS*, 265).

Winthrop's ultimate argument against Hutchinson emerges as a political struggle for survival. According to the governor, the fate of the colony was at stake; Hutchinson threatened to destroy the principle of the state as one body knit together by love. She threatened to divide the state and church into factions that could not even coexist, much less develop into a model community, a holy commonwealth.

Twentieth-century students of the Antinomian Controversy generally find fault with Winthrop. Edmund Morgan, for example, who is generally sympathetic toward the governor, calls the trial "the least attractive episode of Winthrop's career." The documents reveal "a proud, brilliant woman put down by men who had judged her in advance." David D. Hall even maintains that "Mrs. Hutchinson parried the accusations of her examiners with a wit and verve that reduced them to confusion."[12] The consensus appears to be that the controversy stands as a prime indication of the authorities' total intolerance of any belief but their own. According to Philip Gura, however, "the magistrates' and ministers' responses to Anne Hutchinson and her sympathizers must be seen not as a stubborn defense of long-held principles but as the consequence of the colony's process of self-definition."[13]

One of the major threats of Hutchinson, besides her inciting discontent or dissatisfaction with the New England ministers was—according to Winthrop—that if works played absolutely no part in justification, as Hutchinson argued, then godly living, modeling one's behavior on

Christ's, obeying the commandments Moses brought down from Sinai, and even having faith, had no authority whatsoever. For the Puritan, the Scripture was the law; it proscribed life and death. The business of the Puritan ministers was to interpret those texts to the best of their ability for the lay congregation. Hutchinson threatened the whole evangelical principle with its emphasis on the authority of Scripture and the importance of preaching. She challenged the authority of both Scripture and ministers. The patriarchy in the seventeenth century would allow no person, and certainly no woman, to exercise that power.

Winthrop's description of the trial itself constitutes a section of his *Short Story*. Whereas Winthrop briefly summarized the other cases, he gives specific detail of the Hutchinson case, even paraphrasing several of her statements. Winthrop's report is one of very few accounts that is supposed to record Hutchinson's actual words. In the absence of any of her own writing, this account is historically invaluable. Though the court may well have condemned Hutchinson before she entered the Cambridge meetinghouse where her trial was held, Winthrop began by pointing out that the purpose was for her either to acknowledge and reform her faults or to suffer the court's punishment: "that we may take such course with you as you may trouble us no further" (*SS*, 266). The court was trying her, after all, for causing public disturbances; for holding "erroneous opinions"; for broaching those opinions; for encouraging sedition; for "casting reproach upon the faithfull Ministers" and thereby weakening them and raising prejudice against them; and for maintaining public meetings even though the court had explicitly condemned them.

After Winthrop's introductory remark, the court seems to have proceeded in a somewhat unorganized, even haphazard, way. One of the charges brought against Hutchinson concerned her public meetings. The court accused her for teaching, an act reserved in Puritan society exclusively for men. According to Winthrop's account, Hutchinson defended herself by saying that she and her group did no more than "read the notes of our teachers Sermons, and then reason of them by searching the Scriptures." She supported herself by reference to the "men of *Berea* [who] are commended for examining *Pauls* Doctrine" (*SS*, 268). The court's charge, according to Winthrop, was that she did not search Scriptures to confirm, rather she used Scriptures to declare the teacher's meaning or even to correct the teacher. Winthrop condemned the principle of independent thought by members of the congregation because such thought could be dangerous to the homogeneity of the community.

Hutchinson's "ready wit" is evident in her response to the court's challenge that she has no rule from the Bible for teaching as she does:

Court	Yet you shew us not a rule.
Hutch.	I have given you two places of Scripture.
Court	But neither of them will sute your practise.
Hutch.	Must I shew my name written therein? (*SS,* 269)

Winthrop's record of the trial differs here somewhat from the anonymous account of her examination. The discussion, according to that anonymous report, concluded with Winthrop stating that the magistrates would not allow her to hold meetings. She responded that if "it please you by authority to put it down I will freely let you for I am subject to your authority."[14] The difference between the two accounts is significant because it suggests that Winthrop might have allowed his politics to interfere with his record of all the facts. Which account of the trial is closer to the truth remains a mystery because no one can ever know exactly what words were actually spoken in the court, but the comparison reveals that Winthrop might have deliberately decided to omit Hutchinson's submission to his and the court's authority. Winthrop's version does not conceal the fact that Hutchinson was witty, however. It makes clear her ability to argue intelligently with her prosecutors, an ability Winthrop seemed to deny her in his description of her character.

Besides charging her with inciting discontent by her teaching and questioning the doctrine of the Bay ministers, the court accused her of reviling several of the ministers. After excepting Cotton and Wheelwright, she maintained that the New England ministers "could not hold forth a Covenant of free Grace, because they had not the Seal of the Spirit, and that they were not able Ministers of the New Testament" (*SS,* 270). By "seal of the spirit," Hutchinson meant that the new England ministers lacked the figurative mark or seal that signified the permanent indwelling of the Holy Spirit. Without such a seal they were not able ministers of the New Testament and therefore unfit to preach. Winthrop would not tolerate such a reproach of the ministers. According to Winthrop's version, she denied the charge, but the ministers, whom the court had asked to be present for that purpose, affirmed it. After their affirmation, Hutchinson confessed and, according to Winthrop's account, repeated her reproach.

Winthrop's account of the court's proceedings of the following morning portrays the defendant as the antagonist. Hutchinson requested that the ministers "might be sworne to what they had spoken" and declared that an"oath is the end of all controversy" (*SS,* 270). In other words, she simply requested that the ministers take an oath swearing to the truth of their previous testimony. Because they recognized the seriousness of taking such an oath, the ministers were extremely reluctant. If they could not be absolutely sure of what they had said months before, they ran the risk of committing blasphemy. Were they to take the oath and then be proven false, they would surely be liable to the charge of being unworthy ministers, and they would also have broken the third commandment, "Thou shalt not take the name of the Lord thy God in vain, for the LORD will not hold him guiltless that taketh his name in vain" (Exodus 20:7). On this possibility of blasphemy rested Hutchinson's hope.

Whereas the anonymous account records in great detail the arguments over the oath-taking, Winthrop cleverly and politically pauses briefly on this aspect of the trial to state that "All this would not satisfie Mistris *Hutchinson,* but she still called to have them sworne, whereupon the Court being weary of the clamour, and that all mouths might be stopped, required three of the Ministers to take an oath" (*SS,* 271). The chronology of events as Winthrop records them differs significantly from that related in the anonymous account of the examination. According to Winthrop, the oath-taking preceded Hutchinson's confession about her receiving divine revelations. According to the "Examination" record, the ministers did not swear until the very end, that is, not before Hutchinson had already ruined any chance she might have had to obtain the court's leniency or forgiveness. According to Winthrop's chronology, the ministers took their oath just after Cotton's testimony. If this were the case, the ministers would have been taking a much greater risk, and their oaths would have carried more weight. If they did not swear until after Hutchinson described her revelations, the oaths would have been uncontested and therefore virtually meaningless; the defendant was by her own admission by then irremediably convicted.

The account of Cotton's testimony sheds further light on the governor's method of composition. Winthrop is vague on Cotton's actual testimony where it did not seem to fit the court's wishes and conclusions. For example, Cotton stated (according to the anonymous version) that as far as he could recollect, he "did not find her saying they were under a covenant of works, nor that she said they did preach a covenant of works."[15] In a sense Cotton here defended Hutchinson effectively, and any charge on this score would have to be dropped. Ultimately Hutchinson was to convict herself not on the grounds of causing sedition or of overstepping a woman's bounds in teaching and interpreting the scripture, but by revealing that she had a direct spiritual communion with God. Knowing this as he writes his own account of the trial, Winthrop blithely concludes the reference to Cotton's testimony by stating that "Mr. *Cotton* did in a manner agree with the testimony of the rest of the Elders" (*SS,* 271).

The irony of the case against Hutchinson is that even though the court could do little about her teaching, or her being a woman, or her disagreement with the ministers, the court could condemn her for her confession of immediate, divine revelation. Evidently on her own initiative she enumerated the various times she had experienced revelations. Her coming to New England "was revealed" to her as was her knowledge that the magistrates in New England would prosecute her. Of her prosecutors she knew "that for this you goe about to do to me, God will ruine you and your posterity, and this whole State" (*SS,* 273).

Winthrop seems to have been aware of this irony and to have delighted at the opportunity it provided the court to dispose of its arch-enemy with impunity: "Mistris *Hutchinson* having thus freely and fully discovered her selfe, the Court and all the rest of the Assembly (except those of her owne party) did observe a speciall providence of God, that . . . her owne mouth should deliver her into the power of the Court, as guilty of that which all suspected her for, but were not furnished with proofe sufficient to proceed against her" (*SS,* 274). According to Winthrop's account, the governor realized what she was saying when she began, foresaw the inevitable result of such a speech, and so he tried to cut her off: "The Governour perceiving whereabout she went [self-incrimination?] interrupted her . . . but seeing her very unwilling to be taken off, he permitted her to proceed" (*SS,* 271). According to the anonymous "Examination," there is no clue as to when, where, or even if Winthrop tried to stop her from speaking about her immediate revelations.[16]

So speak she did. She spoke until Winthrop could say that "the revelation she brings forth is delusion," and he could have the court cry out in agreement.[17] She proceeded until, as Winthrop narrates it, "The Court saw now an inevitable necessity to rid her away, except wee would bee guilty, not only of our own ruine, but also of the Gospel, so in the end the sentence of banishment was pronounced against her, and shee was committed to the Marshall, till the Court should dispose of her" (SS, 276). As the court passed its sentence, Hutchinson—defeated but still proud and forthright—asked why she was banished. Winthrop replied: "Say no more, the court knows wherefore and is satisfied."[18] Here again Winthrop's version omits this apparent exchange, one that does not show the prosecutor in a very favorable light.

The court may well have been satisfied, for it had just rid itself of the greatest internal threat since the colony's inception in 1630. Whether or not the court was satisfied with Hutchinson's banishment, however, the community had still to deal with Hutchinson's constituency. So although Winthrop had passed the sentence of banishment in November, Hutchinson was allowed to remain, imprisoned in the home of Thomas Weld's brother, in the Boston area (Roxbury) until the season "might be fit, and safe for her departure" (SS, 300). In an effort to shame her even further than the court had done, the elders of the Boston church called her to an excommunication hearing in March 1638. This trial was to be her final humiliation in Boston and a lesson to any who might continue to support her beliefs. The final section of Winthrop's *Short Story* is his account of this church trial.[19]

Hutchinson's confinement through the winter of 1637–38 had not kept her ideas—heresies, according to Winthrop's report—from circulating among some members of the congregations. In vain, several orthodox ministers had visited her in what the ministers maintained were efforts to bring her from her errors. In March the elders of the church sent for her to stand an interrogation. On the Thursday lecture day, 15 March 1638, Anne Hutchinson began her last defense against the commonwealth and the church of Boston. Thursdays were generally set aside as days for public lectures by the clergy. In this sense, Hutchinson's excommunication trial would serve as a public lesson. As Winthrop writes, "she came not into the Assembly till the Sermon and Prayer were ended (pretending bodily infirmity) when she was come, one of the ruling Elders called her forth before the Assembly" (SS, 301).

Winthrop's *Short Story* includes a list of the twenty-nine errors that explain "why the Church had called her." Few of the twenty-nine were ever actually brought up in the sessions preceding her excommunication, but Winthrop maintained the list to be correct, stating that she acknowledged she had spoken all of them. Many of the errors relate to Hutchinson's apparently recent concern with death and resurrection, beginning with the first which reads "That the soules of all men (in regard of generation) are mortall like the beasts" (*SS*, 301).[20] Many of the errors concern body, soul, and spirit and questions about union with Christ at death. Several others in the list have to do more specifically with evidence of grace, and still others concern law and works. For example, in errors 13 and 23, Hutchinson was accused of holding that the laws of Scripture are not binding: "The Law is no rule of life to a Christian," and "We are not bound to the Law, no not as a rule of Life" (*SS*, 302). The repetition suggests the haste with which the errors were drawn up, and the accusation itself hardly seems fair given what is known about Hutchinson's knowledge of and devotion to the Bible.

Winthrop summarizes the two days (the two lecture days the trial lasted), relating that Hutchinson was not entrapped by the ministers who visited her, as she claimed, but that they had come "in compassion to her soule, to helpe her out of those snares of the Devill." The governor, who was in attendance at the trial but who played little part, drew a picture of the accused as stubborn and obstinate; despite the learned ministers' arguments against her opinions, "shee still persisted in her errour, giving forward speeches to some that spake to her" (*SS*, 303, 304).

After a week's recess, Hutchinson returned to the second and last session against her. In the intervening week John Cotton and John Davenport had evidently made some progress with her, for she acknowledged "her error in all the Articles (except the last)" (*SS*, 305). She wrote down her answers to them all. (Alas, that manuscript is lost.) According to Winthrop, she did so well in her responses that "the Assembly conceived hope of her repentance." Such hope was short-lived, however, because many of her answers proved unsatisfactory. Further, writes Winthrop, she argued that she "had not been of that judgement, that there is no inherent reghteousnesse in the Saints." John Cotton gave her over at this point, for despite his admonition the previous week and his long week's conference with her in his home between sessions, she was "maintaining of untruth" (*SS*, 306, 307). Cotton left the matter to her pastor. That pastor, John Wilson, perhaps Hutchinson's most bitter enemy, attacked her viciously. According to the anonymous report of the church trial, he spoke harshly: 'I doe account you from this time forth to be a Hethen and a Publican and soe to be held of all the Brethren and Sisters of this Congregation, and of others. Therefore I *command you* in the name of Christ Jesus and of the Church *as a Leper to withdraw your selfe out of the Congregation.*"[21] So much for a community knit together in a mutual bond of affection. In his version of the church trial, Winthrop did not record Wilson's vituperative final words. The attack, according to Winthrop, was much less vindictive, in that the governor placed blame on Hutchinson herself. Even though she heard some argue on her behalf "that she might have a further respite, yet she herself never desired it" (*SS*, 307). Indeed, Winthrop seems to have been very insistent about having Hutchinson convict and sentence herself.

The governor did set down, without interpretive comment, Hutchinson's final words, however: "In her going forth, one standing at the dore, said, The Lord sanctifie this unto you, to whom she made answer, The Lord judgeth not as man judgeth, better to be cast out of the Church then to deny Christ" (*SS*, 307). Winthrop's motive in including this final outburst might have been to suggest that Hutchinson's former supporters in the Boston congregation had deserted her and turned against her, signifying the total victory of the state and church against such a major and potentially devastating threat as Hutchinson was. Perhaps, too, Winthrop included a description of Hutchinson's exit in this final scene to suggest just how misled the woman was. Certainly in Winthrop's and the church's sense of propriety, Hutchinson was cast out because she seemed to be denying Christ. In the context of Hutchinson's departure, Winthrop did not include the fact that one faithful adherent, Mary Dyer, did rise to join her teacher, nurse, and soul mate as she walked out of the meeting house for the last time.[22]

One can hardly read the history of Anne Hutchinson without the compulsion to feel sorry for her and to want to side with her against the combined forces of the establishments of church and state. The temptation is to see in Hutchinson's trials the noble attributes of a spirit of resistance, an independence of thought, and a pursuit of truth that characterize only a very few. Hutchinson traveled to the New World full of hope and excitement. She had a dream of a holy commonwealth in union with the church just as did the New England patriarchy. The problem was that Hutchinson's vision, conception, and interpretation of that holy commonwealth invited faction, dispute, and the questioning of authority. John Winthrop's vision did not. He rested his hopes on conformity and acceptance of authority. Thus, Hutchinson was to him and his community a dire threat. She had to be disposed of for the good of the colony. Hutchinson was a woman before her time.

With the spring weather in late March 1638, Hutchinson journeyed to Portsmouth—in what is now Rhode Island. There she rejoined her husband and others of her family and friends. Several months later she suffered the miscarriage of a hydatidiform mole,[23] news of which further inspired Winthrop to point out the Lord's displeasure with his former neighbor. In 1642, shortly after her husband's death, Hutchinson and her six youngest children moved to the Dutch settlement on Long Island. The next year she and her family—except for one daughter—were killed by a group of Indians reclaiming the land that European settlers had previously taken from them.

Judging by subsequent journal entries, Winthrop's concern with Hutchinson and her adherents did not end with her banishment and excommunication. Several later journal entries, for example, indicate that the Hutchinson affair had deeply troubled him and his notion of a holy commonwealth. He spent much mental energy trying to justify his actions by recording the divine providences against his antagonist.

The Antinomian Controversy inspired Winthrop to write extensively in various genres. Besides the historical account that was subsequently published as the *Short Story,* he wrote two theological essays, which his friend and guide Reverend Thomas Shepard convinced him not to circulate and which he evidently destroyed. As we have seen, the episode might also have motivated him to write his "Christian Experience" in an effort to convince himself of his own trials, sanctification, and ultimate justification. He engaged in a manuscript debate with Henry Vane in the winter of 1636–37. In May he wrote a tract in defense of the court's order of limiting immigration depending on the immigrants' qualification, following it up with a further defense in response to comments by Vane. In response to many members of the Church of Boston "being highly offended with the governor" for the proceedings of the court against Hutchinson (*J,* 1:256), Winthrop wrote an "Essay Against the Power of the Church to Sit in Judgment on the Civil Magistracy" (November 1637). In the essay Winthrop argues that the "Church hath not power to Call any Civill Magistrate, to give Account of his Juditiall proceedinge in any Court of civill Justice" (*WP,* 3:505). Relying on biblical precedent, he outlines the reasons the church does not and should not have such a power. In his journal history of New England, Winthrop kept track of the developments of the Antinomian Controversy and even reported on Hutchinson's movements after she left the Massachusetts Bay Colony. The journal was to record the important events of the colony.

Chapter Five

The Journal: A History of New England

I would not mention such ordinary matters in our history, but by occasion of some remarkable accidents.

(Winthrop's Journal, 2:43)

Virtually all his adult life, Winthrop kept some form of diary or journal. As we have seen in "Experiencia," he maintained a record of both his spiritual and mundane life as a young man. At nearly fifty, he traced his Christian experiences, perhaps convincing himself of the validity of the process of his conversion. In the spring of 1630, as he began his new life in relation to the New World waiting aboard the *Arbella* for departure for New England, he started a notebook journal in which he would record the history of the Massachusetts Bay Colony. He wrote daily as he crossed the Atlantic and intermittently for the next nineteen years of his life in New England. His incessant scribbling provided posterity three manuscript volumes of the events between 1630 and 1649 that directly influenced and shaped the colony.

Of Winthrop's three original manuscript notebooks, the first and third survive; both are housed in the library of the Massachusetts Historical Society. The second was destroyed by fire. Although several historians had borrowed Winthrop's journals in the years after his death in 1649, no one attempted to publish the work until 1790. William Hubbard (1621–1704) borrowed it in composing his *General History of New England* (1682; published in 1848); Cotton Mather (1663–1728), the namesake and grandson of the Reverend John Cotton, perused it before composing his *Magnalia Christi Americana* (1702). Thomas Prince (1687–1758), pastor of the Old South Church in Boston, may have anticipated using it for a sequel to his *Chronological History of New England* (1736). At any rate the third volume lay undisturbed from 1755 until it was discovered in 1816 in his tower library, where it had providentially escaped burning during America's revolutionary war.[1]

While the third volume lay undiscovered and evidently forgotten,

in 1771 Ezra Stiles (1727–95), former president of Yale College, and
Jonathan Trumbull (1710–85), governor of Connecticut in the 1780s,
transcribed or oversaw the transcription of portions of the first two
volumes. In 1790, without actually seeing the journal itself and relying totally on these transcriptions, the Noah Webster (1758–1843) of
dictionary fame anonymously published a version of Winthrop's journals entitled *A Journal Of the Transactions and Occurrences in the settlement
of Massachusetts and the Other New-England Colonies, from the Year 1630
to 1644: written by John Winthrop, Esq. First Governor of Massachusetts.
And now first published from a correct copy of the original Manuscript.* Webster's text is incomplete and according to Winthrop scholar Richard
Dunn, "marred by many hundred misreadings and omissions."[2] Nonetheless, the beginning of the movement toward publishing the journal
had begun, and an awareness of its value was here made manifest.

Using all three of Winthrop's manuscript volumes, James Savage
(1784–1873), a descendant of Anne Hutchinson, published a two volume edition of the complete history in 1825–26, entitled *The History
of New England from 1630 to 1649. By John Winthrop, Esq. First Governour of the Colony of the Massachusetts Bay. From his Original Manuscripts.*
In 1853 Savage brought forth a second edition. Savage's contributions
are significant. He not only transcribed, edited, and published the
complete journal, he also added copious notes, some extremely helpful,
some quite entertaining. In an effort of questionable value, he also took
it upon himself to modernize the text. The great regret of Savage's
scholarship is that while the second volume of Winthrop's manuscript
was in his possession it was destroyed by fire when the editor's office
burned in 1825. Fortunately, he had already transcribed the entire
volume.

Basing an edition completely on Savage's text, James Kendall
Hosmer published his edition of Winthrop's history as *Winthrop's Journal, "History of New England," 1630–1649* (1908). Like the title, Hosmer's rendition is shorter than Savage's editions. Hosmer reproduced
Savage's text but cut many of the earlier editor's notes, divided the
history into chapters by year, and deleted several passages that he found
distasteful. In omitting the details of Winthrop's description of Anne
Hutchinson's miscarriage he writes that the "repulsive details which
Winthrop took pains to gather are here omitted. They are not inaccessible, and they only show how far bigotry could carry a mind naturally
noble and magnanimous."[3] In another place he simply notes that "Several pages of Winthrop's text are here omitted."[4] In other places he

makes no mention of the omission but indicates each by ellipsis punc-
tuation within the text. In addition to the two deletions concerning
Anne Hutchinson, Hosmer made three cuts, two short and one of several pages, relating the story of an incident of incest.[5] Despite the
deletions, Hosmer's edition is now the most readily available text and
is certainly readable and reliable.

In the 1930s the Massachusetts Historical Society published the first
volume of Winthrop's journal in the *Winthrop Papers*. Here the editorial
policy was to remain as close to the original as possible. The editors
returned to the original manuscript, retaining the seventeenth-century
spelling and noting Winthrop's strike-throughs. They also printed the
map Winthrop drew of the New England coast while aboard the
Arbella.[6]

Despite their indisputable usefulness, these editions of Winthrop's
journal provide but little idea of the actual physical manuscript volumes.[7] The two surviving volumes are covered with vellum, binding
pages that are over 350 years old. Both texts are now understandably
fragile. The first volume is approximately seven by six inches and
barely over an inch thick. The third volume is larger, measuring
roughly ten by six and a half inches. The 169 pages of the first volume
cover the period from March 1630, when Winthrop expected to sail
for New England, until the fall of 1636, the beginning of the Antinomian Controversy. The third volume begins with an entry dated 17
September 1644 and ends with Winthrop's final entry in February
1649, shortly before his death in March.

Besides missing the physical appearance of the journal, the reader
gets no sense of the marvelous chaos of the actual journal. Winthrop's
handwriting itself, "distinctive and devilishly difficult,"[8] gives the
pages the appearance of being indecipherable. One also misses much
of the marginalia. In places the manuscript journal is so beautifully
disorganized that the printed version cannot do it justice. On one manuscript page, for example, Winthrop wrote just four lines of text at the
very top of the page; almost a half page gap follows these lines. The
journalist filled the lower half to the extreme bottom of the page,
leaving no bottom margin whatsoever. In what there is of a left margin
Winthrop wrote four lines vertically.[9] Although this page is not necessarily typical of the manuscript, the method of composition it suggests is not at all rare either.

The entries for July and August 1631 present the editor or reader
with another interesting challenge. In the manuscript Winthrop makes

an entry for 22 July followed by an entry for 21 July. Between the entry for 8 August and 19 August, he writes an entry for 26 July at the top of the page. Winthrop placed a large square bracket in the left margin, evidently to indicate that the entries are out of chronological sequence.[10]

The breaking of the chapters according to the year as Hosmer has done is misleading. Winthrop did not do so. Between the entry for 5 December 1632 and Hosmer's 1 January 1633, for example, the manuscript reveals no break whatsoever.[11] This instance is especially interesting because Winthrop dates his first entry for January (the eleventh month according to Winthrop's calendar) as 9 January 1632.[12] An entry dated 1 January is written in the margin of the manuscript page. The division by year is misleading in a more fundamental way as well; Winthrop's new year occurred in March, not January.

Another feature of the journal not perceived in published editions is the numerous gaps, empty pages, or partial pages. Between the entries for January and February 1634, for example, there are several large gaps between single sentences in the text.[13] One sentence about Isaac Allerton's fishing, for example, is both preceded and followed by a sizable gap.[14] The gaps suggest that Winthrop thought he might return to these passages and either provide the details or record other occurrences for which he did not immediately have the time, the inclination, or perhaps the full knowledge.

For the most part, the manuscript text of Winthrop's third volume is written much more tightly throughout. Almost all of every page is taken up, suggesting, as Dunn has argued, that the governor wrote for longer periods and had a clearer idea of what he was including.[15] Winthrop wrote between thirty-five and forty lines of text per page, twelve to fifteen words per line. There are about 186 manuscript pages in this third volume.

Winthrop's method of composition for the almost twenty years he kept the journal was, as could be expected, somewhat inconsistent. The differences between the opening pages of the first manuscript volume and pages of the third offer a telling contrast. Winthrop began his journal on the day he expected to leave England for the New World: following "Easter Monday," written in the margin, he begins:: "Riding at the Cowes, near the Isle of Wight, in the *Arbella,* a ship of three hundred and fifty tons, whereof Capt. Peter Milborne was master" (*J,* 1:23). For the next two and a half months he made almost daily entries, noting the weather and the ship's bearing. Between 29 March and 14 June he made seventy-eight entries, one for each day. According to Dunn, by "inspecting the manuscript, noting the color of the ink, the thickness of the pen nib, the size of Winthrop's writing, and the slant of his hand, one can tell that he composed this sea journal directly as events occurred."[16] In contrast to this veritable journal (a record comprised of daily entries), Winthrop wrote his third volume as a history, setting down accounts of events after they had occurred: "Inspection of Winthrop's manuscript indicates that he wrote 129 pages of entries in only about fifteen sessions."[17] But one need not study the autograph version of the journals to suspect that the governor's method of composition changed over the years. The early entries are short and come with frequency; the later entries are often long and involve episodes that happened over an extended period of time.

The process of change was gradual and cannot be traced precisely because the second volume no longer exists. The suggestion that Winthrop's journal would eventually turn into a history is already evident, however, in the first manuscript volume. After making an entry for each of the seventy-eight days of the journey across the Atlantic, Winthrop entered nothing for the first three days ashore; the first entry written on New England soil is followed by a two-week gap. He returned to daily entries in July for the first week but then missed almost forty days, not resuming his notebook until 18 August 1630. Certainly the rigors of establishing a colony kept him from his writing. Interestingly, when he did write he made little or no mention of the building of Boston. As to its establishment, he wrote merely that "we went to Mattachusetts, to find out a place for our sitting down" (*J*, 1:50).

The variations in Winthrop's method of composition create an interesting problem in describing the genre of Winthrop's "History of New England." In part it is a journal, a daily record of events as they happen; but it is also a reflective history, a record of facts written after their occurrence and with the advantage of hindsight. Nonetheless, in its method of composition and its style, Winthrop's masterpiece is certainly unlike William Bradford's history *Of Plymouth Plantation*, written several years after the history it records and organized around a specific theme.

In the text itself, at the beginning of the third manuscript volume, Winthrop refers to his work as "the History of New England." The question of genre raised here (and raised by Dunn elsewhere) is significant in a context beyond the naming or titling of an edition of Winthrop's manuscripts.[18] The question is one of deciding how to approach this relic of Americana. Is it merely a private diary? An autobiography? A public journal? To what extent is it a history?

Of its several purposes, one must have been to record God's special providences for the chosen people in New England. Another purpose, as we shall see, seems to have been to provide a positive picture of the colony for the eyes of the rest of the world. We remember that Winthrop felt that all eyes would be upon his city on the hill. Ultimately, in Winthrop's mind, the purpose must have been to chart the course of the holy commonwealth (although it is doubtful whether Winthrop would ever have been so presumptuous as to state it outright), a sequel to Exodus and the story of Canaan.

In many ways as illuminating as what Winthrop chose to include in his journal is what he chose to leave out. For example, he took little space to describe the land, the foliage, the water. He barely mentions the situation of homes around the community and rarely mentions their method of construction. There is little description of the day to day activities of the people he governs. All these are of course earthly, mundane matters and evidently he felt they had no place in the spiritual, holy commonwealth, the building of which he is recording.[19]

Winthrop imposes on the story of his land of milk and honey several themes. Although his journal does not have the thematic clarity of Bradford's history, it does develop themes as it progresses. Bradford's *Of Plymouth Plantation* is noted for its thematic lament of the decline in morals and principles of the Plymouth Separatists. Critics also argue that—despite his awareness of decline—Bradford wrote a history whose theme depends on the cyclic nature of crises and their resolutions.[20] A different type of theme is evident in the journal from Boston. In Winthrop's journal theme is evident, for example, in the stress Winthrop puts on the arrival of ships, on the public-record nature of his journal, and on the difficulty of maintaining a spiritually unified group in and around Boston.

Winthrop's idea of a homogeneous whole was threatened early in his tenure as governor. In the early years, he and his deputy governor, Thomas Dudley, found they could not agree on the proper way to run the government. One possible source of friction between Winthrop and Dudley may owe its genesis to the fact that almost immediately after the emigrants landed in 1630, Dudley built his house in Newtown (Cambridge) under the impression that Winthrop too would build there instead of across the Charles River at Shawmut (Boston). Thomas

Dudley was evidently somewhat jealous of Winthrop's position as governor anyway, and the governor's decision to settle on the peninsula left Dudley outside the center of action.[21] The Charles River presented not only a substantial physical but also a symbolic barrier between Boston and Newtown. As Edmund Morgan suggests, perhaps "Dudley, as deputy governor, was close enough to the throne to be piqued at not occupying it."[22] At any rate, in addition to possibly still being disgruntled about Winthrop's not settling in Newtown, in 1632 the deputy brought charges against Winthrop for assuming too much authority, the type of accusation that would plague the governor throughout his political career.

Dudley complained that Winthrop took too much authority in erecting a fort, in sending gunpowder to Plymouth, in allowing Watertown to erect a weir, in not ridding the community of two banished men; in short, as Winthrop verbalizes the charge, in intending "to make himself popular, that he might gain absolute power, and bring all the assistants under his subjection" (*J,* 1:88). By Winthrop's own account, the governor appears to be capable, wise, temperate, and lenient; perhaps the most admirable of the New England colonists. Dudley, in contrast, appears to be a sniveling, jealous, short-tempered subordinate. Besides giving clear reasons for having taken the authority that he had (supplying Plymouth with gunpowder himself, for example), Winthrop reports that he willingly submitted to the authority and judgment of the court and acknowledged "himself faulty." The accused also defended himself by pointing out that although "the governor might justly have refused to answer" the charges against him, he acted promptly in supplying satisfactory answers "out of his desire for public peace." (*J,* 1:88). According to his own report, the governor gladly paid what the court decided he owed for the maintenance of Newtown's minister. In a magnanimous (and politic) gesture, Winthrop carefully pointed out Dudley's good characteristics; after all, wrote Winthrop, Dudley undertook this action against the governor "in love, and out of his care for the public" (*J,* 1:85). Winthrop's conclusion further dispels any sense of rivalry or malice between the heads of state; they "met about their affairs, and that without any appearance of any breach of discontent, and ever after kept peace and good correspondency together, in love and friendship" (*J,* 1:91). Winthrop's apparently favorable account of total reconciliation between governor and deputy governor is indicative of one aspect of his journal in general. If Winthrop felt he was chronicling a public history of New England, he wanted its leaders to appear amicable. Strife and contention could have no place in the New Canaan.

In this episode Winthrop's purposes were to make a clear record of the misunderstanding between the governor and deputy governor—the two heads of state, as it were—to insure that the record showed discord resolved, and to paint a picture of the governor as tolerant, lenient, and willing to be overruled by the court. If these were indeed his purposes as historian of the Bay Colony, he succeeded.

The troubles between governor and deputy did not end here, but Winthrop here recorded their major quarrel and its resolution. In 1634 Dudley became governor himself (and served again in 1640 and 1645), thus perhaps ending his immediate cause for jealousy. In fact, Winthrop displayed more than a little of his own chagrin about Dudley in his account of that administration. Two journal entries in particular suggest that Winthrop might have been making an effort to deprecate the new governor. On one occasion he recorded that because the governor (Dudley) was not healthy he could not be present at a meeting. In another instance shortly thereafter, Winthrop again noted that Dudley was not present, an absence that prohibited the rest of the company from making a decision concerning Indian policy (see *J,* 1:136, 139).

In 1638 Winthrop described the final reconciliation of the two men by recounting a land-surveying expedition they made. Each offered the other first choice of one thousand acres. They named two "great stones" the Two Brothers, after the fact that they were brothers by the marriage of their children. The naming symbolizes, of course, the brotherhood, peace, and love between them. The episode's inclusion in the journal shows Winthrop's interest in recording harmony among the magistrates.

Winthrop's desire to write the history of a holy commonwealth existing with harmony among the magistrates and ministers was doomed to failure, however, because every season brought new trials for the homogeneity of the commonwealth. One troublesome season was the one that brought Roger Williams (1603–83) to New England. Winthrop's journal provides the fullest and one of the few contemporary accounts of the Bay Colony's trials with the young minister from England.[23] Initially, Winthrop described Williams as a "godly man," praise he reserved for those who had either proven themselves or for whom he had much hope. Williams arrived in Boston in the winter of 1631 on the *Lyon.* He was so well thought of that the Boston church asked him almost immediately to teach in the place of John Wilson, the established minister who was temporarily absent. Williams refused on the grounds that the Boston church had not officially separated itself from the Church of England. This statement of independence marks the beginning of a long and difficult struggle of the state against Roger Williams.

In Salem, Williams received a similar offer to become teacher of the church there, but lost out again on the grounds that his refusal in Boston made him unworthy. Williams went to Plymouth, the home of the Separatists, where he began teaching that the colonists had no right to land granted by a king who "told a solemn public lie, because in his patent he blessed God that he was the first Christian prince that had discovered this land" (*J*, 1:116). For that matter, according to Williams's perception of true Christianity, it was a blasphemy to call Europe the Christian world. Leaving Plymouth in 1633, Williams returned to Salem where he continued to express his disruptive views. The magistrates in Boston got wind of Williams's teachings and brought him before the General Court. The court rebuked Williams and then let him go. Soon he was appearing before the court again, this time because he had taught publicly that tendering an oath to an unregenerate person was taking the Lord's name in vain and therefore a breech of the first table (first four of the Ten Commandments).

Williams's final transgression came in 1635 when he insisted that the Salem congregation dissolve all ties with other churches in the Bay Colony because none of them were true churches. (Plymouth, having its own Patent, was not part of the Massachusetts Bay Colony.) This sedition was more than the magistrates and other Bay ministers would tolerate. The court banished Williams in October 1635. By January the court had decided to ship the troublemaker back to England to ensure that he would cause New England no more trouble, but that plan failed when Captain Underhill arrived to apprehend Williams and found only his empty dwelling.[24]

Despite his vacillating ideas about worship and his threat to the church and state, Williams was evidently a remarkably likeable and persuasive character. Indeed, later evidence suggests that even John Winthrop was taken with his personality and spirit of independence. In a letter written in 1670, many years after his problems with the Boston court, Williams identified Winthrop as one who had encouraged him to avoid being apprehended and sent to England. Winthrop evidently advised him to escape to Narragansett Bay where there was much good he could do.[25] Certainly the correspondence between Winthrop and Williams was frequent and friendly both on public and personal grounds.[26]

Winthrop's journal entries relating to Williams seem especially objective and straightforward. There is little between the lines to suggest that Winthrop abhorred Williams and his doctrines (although he must have feared the political dangers of so public an announcement of separation as Williams advocated). Nor is there much to indicate that Winthrop disliked the man as an individual. The governor did note that one of the reasons to pass over Williams's accusations against the king of England was that they were "written in very obscure and implicative phrases . . . [that] might well admit of doubtful interpretation" (*J*, 1:119). Winthrop seems here to show compassion for the accused. In 1635 Winthrop reported that he found the blackmail the court was attempting to use against the Salem congregation (a grant of land in exchange for Williams's dismissal) to be a "heinous sin" (*J*, 1:155). At this time Winthrop was out of the governorship and so not responsible for the court's underhanded means of ridding the colony of Williams. Were he governor, it seems unlikely that he would have taken such a course, and less likely still that he would have recorded an action of his own as having been a heinous sin. His doing so here suggests both that he might sympathize with Williams and that he is not slow to point out shortcomings of an administration without John Winthrop at its head.

Roger Williams fled to Narragansett Bay and there carried on a correspondence with the governor. Although Winthrop made little mention of Williams's important work with the Indians, he did record the fugitive's work as an intermediary between the colonists and the Indians. One of the good works that Williams found himself able to do at Narragansett Bay was to serve as mediator between the English and the Indians and even between different Indian tribes.

Throughout the journal, Winthrop made notes concerning the English settlers' relationships with the American Indians. He published a tract devoted to troubles with the Indians in 1644, but in his journal he also records the progress and basis of the relationships between colonists and the native Americans.

Concern about the Indians and the company's responsibilities toward them began before the arrival of the *Arbella* in 1630. Before leaving England, in fact, Winthrop expressed his concern for the Indians in his "Arguments for the Plantation." The first argument was that it would be a service to the church to carry the gospel to the Indians. Another concern that received varying degrees of attention was the question of the morality of taking the land that had been for "soe longe tyme possessed by the other sonnes of Adam," the Indians. Williams, too, argued for the Indians' rights to the land. Winthrop answered the objections by stating that there was more than enough land, that Indians could not be said to actually own land anyway, and that "a myraculouse plauge" had decimated the Indian population in the Lord's preparing the way for the English colonists (*WP,* 2:113, 120).

It is impossible to know the sincerity of the colonists' argument about their intention to convert the heathen native Americans, but we must take it as seriously as surviving evidence will allow. Indeed, a few English ministers did make efforts to convert the Indians; John Eliot's efforts or perhaps the most well-known. Whatever their original intentions, however, the English spent more time fearing, fighting, and killing than converting the natives.[27]

Winthrop's journal reflects the colonists' concerns with their new neighbors. He first mentioned the Indians before setting foot on American soil. On 12 June 1630 he noted that an "Indian came aboard us and lay there all night." In the next day's entry Winthrop related that "the sagamore of Agawam and one of his men came aboard our ship and stayed with us all day" (*J,* 1:50). Winthrop clearly intended to demonstrate that the Indians were trustworthy and that the English were making efforts to accommodate rather than antagonize them. The mutual trust that Winthrop described here would serve as good propaganda for any of the potential readers back in England who might hesitate about coming to New England out of a fear of the Indians.

The mutual trust did not last long. By April 1631 Winthrop noted that he had become suspicious and fearful of a Wahginnacut Indian who wished to have two English settlers come to his country with him. Winthrop wrote that he entertained him at dinner "but would send none with him." The governor discovered afterwards that "the said sagamore is a very treacherous man." Winthrop saw both sides of the relationship, however. In October Winthrop noted that even though a company of Indians killed a certain Walter Bagnall, the journalist felt he might have invited death, for he was "a wicked fellow, and had much wronged the Indians" (*J,* 1:61, 69). Winthrop did not send troops to take revenge.

In the fall of 1634 the colonists served as friendly mediators between two warring tribes, the Pequots and the Narragansetts. Winthrop re-

corded that the Pequots wished to make peace and be on friendly terms
with the English in order to trade. The English promised the Narragansetts part of the wampum the Pequots had given as a token of
friendship if the Narragansetts would also keep the peace. The treaty
was put in writing. Winthrop's report shows the English in a most
favorable light, keeping the peace and maintaining law and order. The
English were also introducing Indians to the European custom of a
written peace treaty. Winthrop made no mention, however, of spreading the gospel; instead he wrote of war and trade.[28]

Within two years of this peace-keeping episode, the colony's role
had changed significantly. In July 1636 the Narragansetts killed John
Oldham, who had been trading with the Pequots. In August Henry
Vane, the governor at the time, and the council decided to send ninety
men "to put to death the men of Block Island, but to spare the women
and children." With the death of Oldham, relations with other tribes
of Indians also changed dramatically. The same company that set out
after the Narragansetts had a commission to go to the Pequots "to
demand the murderers of Capt. Stone," using force if necessary (J,
1:186).[29] Winthrop's closing note that "no man was impressed for this
service, but all went voluntaries" is indicative of his theme. The Indians had become a real and dangerous threat to the colonists, dis-
rupting their settlements and trade, and the colony as a whole was
voluntarily willing to fight them. In response to the complaint from
the governor of Plymouth that the Bay colonists provoked the Pequots
but did not conquer them, Winthrop responded with a conclusion that
makes clear the European's sense of superiority in both warfare and
reason. Winthrop argued that the Bay Colony's obviously superior effort against the Pequots would have made them take "notice of our
advantage against them, and would have [encouraged them to sit] still
or have sought peace, if God had not deprived them of common reason." This expression of bigotry is mild, however, in comparison with
Winthrop's ignorance and fear of the Indians in general. He expressed
his fear in the argument that no matter how many Indians the English
would kill, if they "left but one hundred of them living, those might
have done us as much hurt as they have or are likely to" (J, 1:194). In
what it leaves unsaid, this conclusion portends the annihilation of the
native American Indians.

Between the lines it suggests annihilation, but on the surface
Winthrop's text records the efforts the English make to establish peace,
including a list of the very articles of that peace (J, 1:193–94). These

initial relations with the Indians were to have a long and far-reaching impact on the development and settlement of America. The Indians were considered subhuman and lacking in common reason. Further, they were not considered to own land because it was not their custom to own it in the European sense; the English could thus argue themselves into rightfully taking any land and justifying revenge if the Indians made efforts to regain it.[30]

Many of Winthrop's journal entries relating to the Indians from 1636 on are accounts of battles, raids, and attempts to establish policy concerning them as enemies. In May 1637, for example, Pequots killed six men at work, three women, twenty cows, one horse. In July Winthrop wrote that many of the captured Indians were "disposed of to particular persons" (as slaves), and that some of these were "branded on the shoulder." Again in July 1637, the English at New Haven "killed six, and took two. At head of land a little short they beheaded two sachems" (*J*, 1:225–26, 226).

Winthrop's comment concerning the Indian troubles in Virginia indicates his allegiance to New England against not only Indians but against all people and settlements beyond the Bay Colony. He recorded the news of a massacre in Virginia and offers the Indians' rationale: the Indians "saw the English take up all their lands from them, and would drive them out of the country." Further casting aspersions on the Virginians, Winthrop attributed the cause of Virginia's troubles to its ungodliness: "It was very observable that this massacre came upon them soon after they had driven out the godly ministers we had sent to them." He made his point emphatic by recording that the godly among those surviving Virginians came to New England and acknowledged that the massacre "was sent upon them from God for their reviling the gospel" (*J*, 2:167, 168).

Troubles with the Indians were a major concern to the New England colonies, and these concerns play a corresponding large role in Winthrop's journal. Indian troubles, however, were not Winthrop's only war concerns in the early years of the settlement. The French also caused problems because 1) they were enemies of England, the colonists' mother country; 2) they threatened English colonies in the New World by settling to the immediate north; 3) they were Catholic, Papists who according to Puritan tradition were among the worst enemies of Protestant Christians.

Winthrop devoted several journal entries to two Frenchmen in particular, Charles De La Tour and Charles d'Aulnay. Because both men claimed that Louis XIII, king of France until 1643, had offered them the governorship, these two adventurers battled for the control of the French outposts of New Brunswick and Nova Scotia. This struggle motivated La Tour to turn to New England, and on a quest for help he sailed unimpeded into Boston Harbor.

Though there had been one French raid against the English in the early 1630s, later the trade relations between the two colonies were friendly. Winthrop's real involvement with the French began in June 1643, when La Tour sailed to Boston "to crave aid to convey him to his fort" (*J,* 2:106), the entrance to which D'Aulnay was blocking.[31] Winthrop described the episode of La Tour's visit in great detail, apparently in an effort to justify his action of unofficially siding with La Tour. Winthrop's official word, of course, was that the colonists could not side with either La Tour or D'Aulnay because to side with either would be to risk war with the French state.

Winthrop reasoned that La Tour might be trustworthy and therefore deserving of the Bay Colony's support because he had had the opportunity to make a surprise attack on Boston, but he had not attacked. The commonwealth had abandoned the castle protecting the harbor; La Tour had the governor and his family isolated at the governor's garden outside Boston, yet La Tour entered the harbor peacefully. The Frenchman could have taken the ships in the harbor with little or no resistance, and because he did not do so, Winthrop drew the conclusion that "his neglecting this opportunity gave us assurance of his true meaning" (*J,* 2:106). The magistrates decided that they could not supply La Tour as an ally but suggested that he might hire as many men and ships as were willing to accompany him to quarrel with D'Aulnay. La Tour readily agreed to these terms.

The next problem arose when Winthrop allowed La Tour's troops to exercise on the common, an open field where the colonists practiced their own military actions. The ministers questioned the propriety of Winthrop's entertaining the French, and the journal records the consequent debate. Questions arose concerning whether it would be "lawful for Christians to aid idolaters" (*J,* 2:109) and whether it would be safe for the colony to allow the French to exercise with weapons so close to home. Because they were Catholics, the French were in Puritan eyes a great enemy of the Protestant community. As was typical of Puritans, the magistrates and elders turned to passages from Scripture to make their arguments.

Winthrop dutifully recorded the arguments for and against aiding

La Tour. He refers to Jehoshaphat, an ally to Ahab who was deemed ungodly, Josias who aided Babylon, and Amaziah for hiring an army out of God's Israel. In each case Winthrop answered that the biblical precedent did not quite apply to the present situation with the French. He also argued that—although by "aiding papists" the colonists "advance and strengthen popery,"—he hoped to weaken popery "by winning some of them to the love of the truth." Hosmer calls this a "labored argument fortified pro and con by far-fetched Biblical precedents."[32] In his argument against risking war with France or D'Aulnay, Winthrop conceded that "Papists are not to be trusted, seeing it is one of their tenets that they are not to keep promise with heretics," an interesting statement of the reciprocal distrust and disapproval of each other's brand of Christianity (*J*, 2:110).

Winthrop's method here as elsewhere supported his position. The colony had lent support to La Tour by allowing him to hire ships and men, so Winthrop's post facto argument was his rationalization for having given that support. Organizing his response accordingly, he introduced his arguments against aiding La Tour and for each gave his logical answer. Beginning the "arguments on the affirmative," he admitted that many were "touched in the former answers" to the arguments against the aid (*J*, 2:113). As a good rhetorician, Winthrop argued with a sophistry that merits praise regardless of one's stance on the issue. Winthrop's purpose was twofold. He wanted to record the event as part of the history of New England and at the same time to defend the colony's actions as admirable, taken in the best interest of the colony, and acceptable to the Lord who was thought to watch so carefully over the commonwealth.

The summer following La Tour's visit, the magistrates reiterated their questions, wondering whether "it were lawful for true Christians to aid an antichristian" and whether it would be safe to support La Tour. As it turned out, the colony was under little danger from D'Aulnay, the eventual victor who forced La Tour to become a "pirate." La Tour's metamorphosis proved to Winthrop "(as the scripture saith) that there is no confidence in an unfaithful or carnal man" (*J*, 2:275). D'Aulnay remained a minor threat to traders. In March 1647, for example, Winthrop recorded that the Frenchman took and kept one a Boston merchant's ship (See *J*, 2:322–23). But the court decided that D'Aulnay was within his rights and reprisal would be unjust. Again Winthrop demonstrated his political sophistication in staying out of trouble with the French. In keeping his journal record of the events, he justified New England's policies and actions to any contemporary or future would-be detractors.

In addition to finding room in his history for the troubles with the Indians and the threat of the French, Winthrop found room to record internal problems and problems with England. During the last few years of his life, he duly recorded events that threatened New England, continually developing the theme that despite all the Devil's attempts, the holy commonwealth in the New World would survive.

In 1643 Winthrop recorded the beginnings of an episode between the General Court and Samuel Gorton that would threaten both the colony's religious unity and its political independence for several years. Gorton had arrived in Boston in 1638 armed with what the established colonists considered heretical, anabaptist notions. He was not prominent in Winthrop's eyes, however, until he caused problems in Patuxet near Providence, Rhode Island, in 1643. After some epistolary and martial exchanges between the two parties, the General Court captured, tried, and punished Gorton for his dissidence. Eventually Gorton took his case to England where he presented it to the Commission for Foreign Plantations, a parliamentary committee that decided in his favor that the Massachusetts Bay colonists indeed had no right to interfere with a settlement outside the boundaries of the Bay Colony. The committee's decision was of crucial importance to Winthrop because it proved that a colonist could successfully appeal a case in England and because it demonstrated that Parliament could interfere with governmental business in New England.[33]

Although in 1643 when he made the entry Winthrop could not have known how serious Gorton's supposed subversiveness would become, he took extreme care to couch his response to the affair in rhetorically safe language. It was only on "the complaint of the English of Patuxet . . . who had submitted to our jurisdiction" that the Bay Colony interceded. And even then it was only after the complainants had suffered "continual injuries" that the court sent a letter. The letter itself was "not in a way of command" but a mere request. After acknowledging the need for force, Winthrop wrote with the relatively rare use of first person, "we would hear their answers." In relating the skirmish, Winthrop concluded that it "was a special providence of God that neither any of them nor of ours were slain or hurt, though many shot passed between them, but every man returned safe and hale" (J, 2:139, 141).

In 1645 a group of congregationalists from the town of Hingham accused Winthrop of overstepping his authority, and they demanded the court's ear on the matter. The trouble started innocuously enough. The townspeople chose "one Allen to be their captain," replacing the former lieutenant, Anthony Emes. The General Court stepped in and the magistrates, "considering the injury that would hereby accrue to Emes," refused to allow Bozoun Allen to become the militia captain (*J*, 2:229). Afterwards, the Hingham troops refused Allen's bid to take charge on training day. Mutiny ensued.

Although Dudley was governor at the time, the affair seems to have fallen into Winthrop's lap for—as he recorded it—it was the deputy who labored to straighten out the confusion (See *J*, 2:232). (That the accusations were brought against Winthrop rather than Dudley suggests the extent to which he was in charge despite his status as deputy governor.) As reward for his efforts, the Hingham petitioners singled out Winthrop as the one to charge with having overstepped his authority. Again standing accused, Winthrop carefully declared that the petitioners were out of order to demand a magistrate "to answer criminally in a cause, wherein nothing of that nature could be laid to his charge." He accepted the challenge, however, and agreed to a public hearing, "knowing well how much himself and the other magistrates did suffer in the cause, through the slanderous reports (*J*, 2:232, 233). The public hearing was agreed upon.

Winthrop's description of himself and his actions shows how he gained psychological advantage over his opponents by presenting himself as a criminal. "The deputy governor, coming in with the rest of the magistrates, placed himself beneath within the bar, and so sate uncovered. Some question was in the court about his being in that place (for many both of the court and the assembly were grieved at it). But the deputy telling them, that, being criminally accused, he might not sit as a judge in that cause." As it appears in Winthrop's account, then, the accused put his attention not on the charge against him but on his response, turning the charge to his advantage: "he accounted it no disgrace, but rather an honor put upon him, to be singled out from the brethren in the defense of a cause so just . . . and of so public concernment" (*J*, 2:233). Again he pointed out the irregularity of the petitioners' method for singling him out as one of the whole court, and for accusing him criminally when he had done nothing criminal. Rhetorically, too, Winthrop vindicates himself, and the journal again describes the authorities in the commonwealth as just, honorable, and righteous.

The Hingham mutineers' petition occasioned what has come to be known as Winthrop's "little speech" on liberty. Winthrop made the speech at the conclusion of the hearing, and in it he sets forth his theory of liberty. That speech and the theory it embodies demonstrate as much as any other piece of writing Winthrop's political beliefs. The speech deserves separate attention and is discussed in another chapter. After Winthrop was acquitted "legally and publicly" of all that was charged against him (*J*, 2:237), the court fined the petitioners and admonished Emes. Once again Satan's bid to slither into New England was frustrated.

That the affair did nothing to affect the respect the majority of freemen had for Winthrop is evidenced by his election as governor once again the following spring. After his reelection in 1646, Winthrop immediately faced another potentially devastating threat to the colony. One of Winthrop's final major trials, then, was an episode that received special attention in his journal, the remonstrance and humble petition Robert Child and William Vassall submitted to the court in May 1646.

The motivation behind the Remonstrance of 1646 was undoubtedly complex, but it essentially asked the Massachusetts Bay government to grant rights to those colonists who were not members of a New England congregation and who therefore were denied certain rights and privileges. These nonfreemen (nonchurch members) wanted the rights they would have had in England and felt they deserved as Englishmen. The petitioners pointed out that without a written body of laws English emigrants were unenfranchised in that they could not vote or hold office, nor were they part of any New England congregation even though they were legitimate members of the Church of England. In essence, Child and the others who signed the petition asked the magistrates to open their arms to a great number of nonchurch members. Child's request harks back to the law that Winthrop and the original General Court enacted in 1630. The court proposed to allow the freemen (all free, male, full members of the church) to choose the assistants. Once chosen, the assistants would select a governor and deputy governor from amongst themselves. Child was a freeman but not a full member of the church and was therefore ineligible to vote or hold office. According to the court's interpretation, the charter gave rights only to those who were church members.[34]

Broaching the subject of the remonstrance in his journal, Winthrop describes the antagonist Vassall before narrating the details of the court's dealings with Child and the other remonstrancers. He describes Vassall as "a man of a busy and factious spirit, and always opposite to the civil governments of this country and the way of our churches" (*J*,

2:271). Winthrop interprets the remonstrance as the petitioners' desire that the colony "might be wholly governed by the laws of England" rather than that it maintain the distinctions in government granted by the charter.[35]

The following November, in conjunction with the problem of Samuel Gorton's appeal in London, the members of the court considered Child's petition serious enough to merit their sending "some able man into England" to represent the Bay Colony's interests. In his typical third-person narrative style, Winthrop writes that the "governor was very averse to a voyage into England, yet he declared himself ready to accept the service if he should be called to it" (*J*, 2:289, 295). Perhaps in deference to Winthrop's age, the court chose to send Edward Winslow of Plymouth as its representative in England. In this session the magistrates also considered the Bay Colony's relation to England and established a consensus as to its self-sufficiency, agreeing that a new charter would not be desirable. Winthrop includes the texts of several documents in his history, among them the elders' advice concerning the question of dependence on England and the committee's twelve-part charge against Child and the other petitioners. He also includes a point-by-point account of the petitioners' answers to the charge and the court's replies to those answers.

In the context of the remonstrance, Winthrop's journal provides an excellent firsthand account of the Child affair both by providing documents and by narrating, in some cases minutely, the actions of the court and the petitioners. Indeed, the governor's account reads like a history; virtually the whole episode is presented in one uninterrupted section of the journal. Winthrop recorded another victory for the Bay Colony against the satanic forces, a victory that kept the churches as the magistrates wanted them and indicated that the Bay colonists could keep the English Parliament from interfering with New England politics. Once again, Satan was defeated on the shores of Massachusetts. And in a special providence of God, Child's supporters were tossed and troubled at sea.

In addition to making history for New England, the remonstrance provided Winthrop with an opportunity to point out the providences of God concerning the righteousness of the colony's actions. One of the petitioners, Thomas Burton, "continued in great pain and lame divers months" because of a fall he took shortly after Child's trial (*J*, 2:317). This same Burton had suggested himself the providential nature of several mishaps suffered by Edward Winslow and his family. In a battle

of providences, however, Winthrop quickly gained the upper hand, for
in December he observes "a special providence of God pointing out his
[God's] displeasure against some profane persons, who took part with
Dr. Child, etc., against the government and churches here" (*J*, 2:321).
And again in 1648 Winthrop wrote about "how the hopes and endeavors of Dr. Child and other petitioners, etc. had been blasted by the
special providence of the Lord" (*J*, 2:339).

Despite the governor's penchant for elaborating on the providences
of God showing New England in favorable light, Winthrop's journal
is unquestionably the fullest single contemporary source of information
on the early history of Boston. With few exceptions his accounts are
verified by other contemporaneous accounts. But his journal is not
merely the historical account of the colony; it is also a work of literature
in that it captures the timelessness of its subjects' beliefs, hopes, fears,
triumphs, and defeats.

Chapter Six

The Journal: A New Literature for a New World

In the meantime most of our people went on shore upon the land of Cape Ann, which lay very near us, and gathered store of fine strawberries.

(Winthrop's Journal, 1:50)

As a history of the first twenty years of the Massachusetts Bay Colony in New England, Winthrop's journal is invaluable. Indeed, many historians have utilized Winthrop's journal extensively as one of the major sources for the early history of the colony. In the surge of attention to its merit as history, however, critics have paid surprisingly little attention to the work for its own sake. Richard Dunn, like other editors before him, has written about the composition of the journals and has compared Winthrop's journal with other, contemporary histories of settlements in the New World.[1] Barbara McCrimmon has written briefly about the publication history and has discussed some of the topics of Winthrop's journal.[2] In her study *Before the Convention,* M. Susan Power describes Winthrop's journal and discusses its symbolic content in relation to his sermon "A Modell of Christian Charity," arguing that whereas the "Modell" theorizes about a preconceived system, the journal records Winthrop's actual, ultimately vain efforts to build the commonwealth the shipboard lay-sermon promised.[3]

Winthrop's journal does seem to have a purpose beyond the mere recording of the first twenty years of the Massachusetts Bay Colony. Perry Miller formulated a definite purpose for Winthrop and his contemporary New England historians. According to Miller, "the entire purpose of the New England historians [was to] chronicle the providence of God in the settlement of New England."[4] Whether or not Miller is guilty of overgeneralization, the story Winthrop tells in his journal is undeniably permeated with ideas and the exposition of values reaching beyond the mere record of fact. Winthrop's journal both records the triumphs and calamities of an entire community and the-

matically reports one writer's hopes, trials, successes, and disappoint-
ments. Winthrop's "History of New England," as he characterized the
journal himself on the first page of the third volume, is one important
marker on the path that leads to a distinct American literature.

If trials are to be a major subject and overcoming them a theme,
Winthrop's opening entries are certainly appropriate. The first major
trial the writer faced was to cross the Atlantic Ocean. The journal
opens with a minute account of the sea crossing, so minute in fact that
Charles Banks was able to use it to chart what he supposes to be the
actual route the *Arbella* and the rest of the fleet took in the spring of
1630.[5] As new as the sea venture was to the Puritans, Winthrop evidently did have a model for his description of an Atlantic crossing.
After journeying to New England a year earlier, Francis Higginson had
sent back to England his "True Relation of the Last Voyage to New
England" (1629), and Winthrop seems to have had a copy of it sent to
his wife at Groton.[6] On 8 April 1630 after a week's delay in the waters
off Southampton, the *Arbella* set sail.

As Banks's account demonstrates, part of Winthrop's purpose must
have been to provide a document by which subsequent voyagers could
navigate the Atlantic, but he also provided a help to later emigrants
in understanding the perils and knowing what to expect in crossing
the sea, such as attacks from enemy or pirate vessels, storms, and
calms. Beyond these pragmatic functions, Winthrop's sea-journal provides a fascinating account of a landsman's concerns while at sea for the
first time. Perhaps most striking is the landlubber's obsession with the
wind. All but one of the seventy-eight entries in the sea-journal mention the wind—the lifeblood, as it were, of a seventeenth-century
ocean-going ship. Not only did Winthrop's immediate physical safety
depend upon the wind, but so did the future of his colony. Thus it is
not surprising that of the entries Winthrop wrote at sea, all mention
the wind, all but about five begin with a description of the wind, and
many entries deal exclusively with the wind and weather.[7]

After threats from supposed enemy vessels, storms, and calms, the
sea-weary Puritans sighted land on 6 June 1630. On 12 June, Winthrop fails to mention wind for the first time during the voyage:
"About four in the morning we were near our port" (*J*, 1:49).[8] Now
that the wind had brought ship and passengers safely across the Atlantic to the New England garden, Winthrop must have felt that he was
near his new home and that the wind was not the major concern it had
been for the previous eleven weeks.

The wind was both friend and foe, friend as it carried the *Arbella* and other ships safely across the Atlantic, foe as it also brought with it deadly storms or withheld itself in equally threatening calms. From the shore, Winthrop characterizes the weather as another antagonist in his narrative of the colony. In the early years, he wrote repeatedly of the severe New England storms, heat waves, and cold spells. The first winter seems to have been particularly extreme. In February Winthrop recorded the freezing of the rivers, boating mishaps, deaths due to weather, and the severity of the wind: "this day the wind came N.W., very strong, and some snow withal, but so cold as some had their fingers frozen, and danger to be lost" (*J*, 1:55). In August 1632, Winthrop recorded a tempest that prevented sailing. The summer was "wet and cold" (*J*, 1:89). The summer and fall of 1634 were evidently hot and dry. The following winter is remembered by an "extraordinary tempest of wind and snow." Indeed, "the weather was many times so tedious as people could not travel" (*J*, 1:143). Winthrop reports that hurricanes would occasionally threaten destruction as well. In one instance he records the uprooting of trees, overturning of houses, and the grounding of ships. Winthrop peppers his journal with such reports, indicating that one of the many obstacles the valiant colonists had to overcome was adverse weather. There is never any doubt, however, that with God's help overcome it they will. After one particularly vicious storm, for example, Winthrop writes that "there did appear a miraculous providence in their preservation" (*J*, 1:156).

Turning from the Atlantic crossing and the weather, Winthrop found room in his journal to record that "there came a smell off the shore like the smell of a garden." Shortly after the passengers came within reach of the land they had been yearning for, Winthrop continued the garden imagery in a description of the passengers leaving ship: "most of our people went on shore upon the land of Cape Ann, which lay very near us, and gathered store of fine strawberries" (*J*, 1:47, 50).

As paradisaical as these entries are, Winthrop provided few descriptions of this newfound paradise in the following months. Shortly after arriving, he took up the business of beginning a city from scratch, an endeavor that seems to have taken all his time and energy; the journal is blank concerning the details about the settling of Boston, just as it had been blank concerning life aboard a ship. What the passengers did with their time or the governor with his must be projected from consideration of other accounts. Winthrop gave little space to the mundane projects of building houses, planting crops, and setting out

gardens. He neglected the mundane because he intended to create a
public record of the settling of a holy commonwealth, and he hoped to
provide political propaganda for the enhancement of the colony. Certainly it was important to him to record the moral and religious aspects
of the settlement, not the daily activities of mere mortal men and
women. An implied theme of the journal seems to be that despite all
the trials that the colonists were to face in coming years, Winthrop's
opus would assert the colony's success. Each potentially cataclysmic
threat would be introduced, overcome, and disposed of. Even though
Satan is always at work, Winthrop would write, the commonwealth
would pursue its course in becoming that city on a hill.

Consistent with the public-document nature of the journal, the governor's first entries after the arrival of the *Arbella* record the coming of
the other ships, whose safe arrivals were certainly seen to be a positive
omen for the establishment of the colony. Indeed, after listing the
week's arrivals, Winthrop noted that the company "kept a day of
thanksgiving in all the plantations" (*J*, 1:51). The list of arrivals also
anticipated a matter that was to become crucial to the colony, that of
emigration. The arrival of ships for the first few years meant more
colonists, bringing money and buying the goods the New Englanders
could provide them. The more the arrival of ships helped the community, the more important it was for Winthrop to record the fact. In
this way the journal becomes a public statement of the colony's economic self-sufficiency.

In the first months Winthrop recorded arrivals, deaths, fires, boating mishaps, and severity of the weather. He did not create his first
extended narrative until December 1630 when he tells of an accident
at sea. The entry immortalizes Richard Garrett, a shoemaker, by recounting the story of his attempt to sail to Plymouth in midwinter.
After shipwreck caused by ice and severe weather, Garrett and most of
the boat's party died of exposure or frostbite. With this account,
Winthrop ushered in what was to become one of the most distinctive
characteristics of his journal, the narrative with an implied or merely
insinuated moral. In this case since the shoemaker had attempted to
make his journey "against the advice of his friends," the narrative reiterates Winthrop's emphasis on the importance of people banding and
staying together. The same might be said for the colony as a whole.
Returning to Boston, Garrett's daughter's "boat was well-manned, the
want whereof before was the cause of their loss" (*J*, 1:55, 56).

The notion of being well-manned in the New England wilderness is a theme Winthrop seemed to think he could not stress forcefully enough. One of the conditions of immigration, according to the Cambridge Agreement written and signed in England in 1629, was that the commitment to come to New England was binding because each member of the new community depended desperately on all the others. Therefore, Winthrop could not tolerate those who chose to return to England or leave the Bay Company's jurisdiction. To a large extent, Winthrop avoided even mentioning colonists' departures or their desire to depart, but in one instance he notes how even the thought of better times in old England could be dangerous: "It hath been always observed here, that such as fell into discontent, and lingered after their former conditions in England, fell into the scurvy and died" (*J*, 1:58).

If merely thinking about the comforts of a former home in England could result in scurvy or death, actually deserting by traveling back to the mother country could invite catastrophe: "Of those which went back in the ships this summer, for fear of death or famine, etc., many died by the way and after they were landed, and other fell very sick and low" (*J*, 1:58). Winthrop here early established a theme that would recur throughout the history. He lamented the departure of members of the colony. Since such departures did not speak well for the community, he rarely mentioned them except to note the misfortune that befell the deserters. The New England patriot must have been especially upset at the hastening away of John Humfrey, four ministers, and a schoolmaster in December 1641. In September 1642 he records the trials of their voyage back to England with this preface: "The sudden fall of land and cattle, and the scarcity of foreign commodities, and money, etc., with the thin access of people from England, put many into an unsettled frame of spirit, so as they concluded there would be no subsisting here, and accordingly they began to hasten away, some to the West Indies, others to the Dutch, at Long Island . . . and others back for England." For those who abandoned the godly enterprise in New England, Winthrop had little sympathy. Indeed, he seems almost to have thrived on their misfortune, writing that although it "pleased the Lord to spare their lives . . . yet the Lord followed them on shore. Some were exposed to great straits and found no entertainment, their friends forsaking them. One had a daughter that presently ran mad, and two other of his daughters, being under ten years of age, were discovered to have been often abused by divers lewd persons, and filthiness in his family. The schoolmaster had no sooner hired an house, and gotten in some scholars, but the plague set in, and took away two of his own children" (*J,* 2:82–83).

Besides describing the dangers of defecting and returning to England, Winthrop also recorded information about other colonies in America, those both near and far. He reported each colony's shortcomings and presented each as altogether unappealing. Of Virginia, for instance, he writes that the custom was to be "usually drunken," and even formerly godly ministers gave themselves up to "pride and sensuality" (*J,* 2:20–21). In incidents closer to home, Winthrop also seems to emphasize the negative aspects of a particular community, if it in any way threatens the unity, homogeneity, or progress of his own Bay Colony. His accounts of the Reverend Thomas Hooker's experiences in Connecticut are a case in point. As early as September 1634 Hooker and his company desired to resettle in Connecticut. Winthrop, deputy governor at the time, opposed their removal for the same reasons he regretted the departure of any group beneficial to the commonwealth: "in point of conscience, they ought not to depart from us, being knit to us in one body, and bound by oath to seek the welfare of this commonwealth" (*J,* 1:132). Although through his arguments he was able to thwart an immediate departure, he could not prevent Hooker and his congregation from eventually leaving and settling on the Connecticut River in what is now Hartford. Winthrop records Hooker's departure on 15 October 1635. At the very top of the manuscript page he writes that the sixty people went to Connecticut and, "after a tedious and difficult journey, arrived safe there" (*J,* 1:163). The journey may well have been as tedious as Winthrop reports, but the author's disgruntlement at their departure seems to have colored his report. Following this entry, Winthrop left almost half a page blank, suggesting he had more to say on the matter, but that he never got back to it.

Winthrop did get around to reporting the Connecticut colony's misfortunes, however. In the first winter those colonists lost two thousand pounds' worth of cattle and had to subsist on "acorns, and malt, and grains." Later he added that "Things went not well at Connecticut." (*J,* 1:178, 200). Even though he forgave Hooker completely and praised him sincerely at his death (*J,* 2:326–27), he still managed to point out the tribulations suffered by Hooker's community and to compare that community unfavorably with Boston. Winthrop's thematic implication is that those who leave the Bay Colony will be punished for their transgression. Such punishment is attributed to God who was most certainly, in the eyes of the colonists, watching carefully over Boston as a holy commonwealth.

Winthrop also turned to his journal to map the progress of Anne Hutchinson, a much more threatening transgressor. The beleaguered governor depended on his occasional entries to demonstrate that the Lord continued to be displeased with her after her banishment and excommunication. Winthrop reported that her miscarriage "might signify her errour in decrying inherent righteousness."[9] Winthrop's detailed account of the physician's report was his way of demonstrating how Anne Hutchinson was pertinaciously pursued for her troublemaking in Boston. In 1639 Winthrop mentioned that there were political troubles at Aquiday, Hutchinson's place of settlement (*J*, 1:299). In 1641 he reported that civil and ecclesiastical unrest was great, causing a great schism among them. In Boston Hutchinson's son and son-in-law were both troublemakers (*J*, 2:39–41). The implication is, of course, that any place where Hutchinson settled would suffer, as would anybody related to or in sympathy with her. In 1638 Winthrop exclaimed that those who went with Hutchinson "fell into new errors daily," a falling that God-fearing Bostonians would want to avoid at all costs. Outsiders would know that Hutchinson was corrupt and corrupting. He also reported that she still suffered from delusions: "By these examples we may see how dangerous it is to slight the censures of the church; for it was apparent, that God had given them up to strange delusions" (*J*, 1:284, 297).

In reporting Hutchinson's death by Indians the journalist reminded his readers that these "people had cast off ordinances and churches" and noted that after the deaths of her and her family "a good providence of God" saved some of the others in her community (*J*, 2:138). Finally, as late as 1646, eight years after the Antinomian Controversy had passed, Winthrop suggested that Hutchinson's children continued to suffer punishment for their mother's transgressions. A daughter who escaped death at the hands of the Indians was eventually returned to the colonists, but she "had forgot her own language, and all her friends, and was loath to have come from the Indians" (*J*, 2:276–77). The description suggests that as a final punishment for the sins of her mother this daughter lost her language and very identity in New England, from Winthrop's perspective a grave punishment indeed.

Certainly one of the major functions of Winthrop's journal (as suggested in the previous chapter) was for Winthrop to write down for

posterity a record of the history of the Massachusetts Bay Colony. To
this end he detailed not only his response to Hutchinson but also to
other major threats to the community; he recorded the court sessions
and the community's successes and failures. Depending on context,
however, he related episodes emphasizing varying details. Indeed, one
of the aspects of Winthrop's journal that makes it enjoyable reading as
well as informative history is the inclusion of many brief accounts from
the experiences of the colonists. His large history includes numerous
small private histories, many of which Winthrop related with a special
knack for the art of story-telling. There are, in fact, so many delightful
vignettes that choosing from among them is itself difficult and any
selection must be somewhat arbitrary. But any selection shows that
Winthrop became a good storyteller.

Perhaps the most famous, certainly one of the most frequently an-
thologized, parables is his story of the battle between the snake and
the mouse: "At Watertown there was (in view of divers witnesses) a
great combat between a mouse and a snake; and, after a long fight, the
mouse prevailed and killed the snake. The pastor of Boston, Mr. Wilson, a very sincere, holy man, hearing of it, gave this interpretation:
That the snake was the devil; the mouse was a poor contemptible people, which God had brought hither, which should overcome Satan
here, and dispossess him of his kingdom" (*J*, 1:83–84).

The account is indicative of Winthrop's story telling in several ways.
As a historian, Winthrop recorded fact. Here he insured the reader's
faith in this verity of the matter by noting the several witnesses. The
episode has a meaning that a sincere and holy person could interpret
according to God's intentions for New England or for the settlers in
the new colony. This account differed from Winthrop's typical accounts
in the length to which the narrator went (via Wilson's interpretation)
to explain the moral. More often Winthrop only inferred the moral or
stated it briefly as God's providence for New England.

A parable with a less obvious message is that of a poor Mr. Mansfield
and a rich Mr. Marshall, a story which is "a witness of God's providence
for this plantation." As Winthrop narrates it, Mansfield wanted badly
to come to New England but could not afford the passage for himself
and his family. Since Marshall, the wealthy merchant, was troubled by
bad dreams about the poor man, he gave him fifty pounds and lent
him another one hundred, enabling Mansfield to sail to New England.
Winthrop concludes by stating that this "Mansfield grew suddenly

rich, and then lost his godliness, and his wealth after" (*J*, 1:141).

This seemingly cryptic passage suggests the complexity of Winthrop's art. If the emphasis falls on the final sentence, God, through providence, appears to intend the immigrant Mansfield to lose his godliness and wealth after getting to New England. Another possibility, one that seems more likely in light of Winthrop's general purpose, is that God's providence for the colony is made evident through Mansfield's receipt of the means to travel to New England in the first place. Winthrop implies that God provides for the colony, and at the same time suggests that the snare of worldly wealth threatens even those sometimes shown God's favor. Because of God's high expectations for the New England colonists, their corruption is especially lamentable. So much for Mansfield. By God's providence he got to New England; by his own fault he let Mammon corrupt him; and he is punished for his corruption by losing his new wealth.

The moral of a story about a woman who attempted to drown her infant is much more obvious, yet the story seems equally complex. "A woman of Boston congregation, having been in much trouble of mind about her spiritual estate, at length grew into utter desperation, and could not endure to hear of any comfort, etc., so as one day she took her little infant and threw it into a well, and then came into the house and said, now she was sure she should be damned, for she had drowned her child; but some, stepping presently forth, saved the child" (*J*, 1:230). This short narrative demonstrates the power that concern about personal salvation had over the colonists. Writing it in the midst of the Antinomian Controversy (summer 1637), Winthrop demonstrates the problems that result from controversies about justification. The narrator implies that such church problems, which should never have existed to begin with, result in tragic actions. The moral is so obvious for Winthrop and his readers that he evidently felt no need to enunciate it. Mortals can never truly know their spiritual estate; therefore, it is pointless to challenge God in an attempt to determine that estate. Winthrop depicts, by means of this woman, a person's helplessness to establish or verify her own damnation. Winthrop's unstated lesson is that because men and women can not know their estate on earth they should not fail to live by the rules of God and the Bible, its being the only testament they have of God's workings. In another similar incident concerning a mother who unsuccessfully attempts to drown her child, Winthrop does conclude his tale with a moral: "Thus doth Satan work by the advantage of our infirmities, which should stir us up to cleave the more fast to Christ Jesus and to walk the more humbly and watchfully in all our conversation" (*J*, 2:61).

Winthrop did not always leave the moral of his parables up to his reader's interpretations. In a story about a godly woman who "set her heart too much upon" a "parcel of very fine linen of great value" and who consequently had to suffer its accidental loss, the historian states the obvious moral for his readers: "but it pleased God that the loss of this linen did her much good, both in taking off her heart from worldly comforts, and in preparing her for a far greater affliction by the untimely death of her husband, who was slain not long after" (*J*, 2:30–31).

Judging by the frequency of entries, perversion of the socially sanctioned sex drives of men and women was a subject that evidently fascinated Winthrop. Such perversion could manifest itself in adultery, licentiousness, incest, and even bestiality. To Winthrop all such perversions were obvious signs of Satan's continual work to corrupt the godly and undermine the sanctity of the holy commonwealth. In an episode that exemplifies the depths of the colonists' beliefs in what would now be considered superstition, Winthrop records the story of a "loose fellow in the town" who—because of some "human resemblances" between the man and a pig—is suspected of fathering a sow. When questioned, the suspect confessed and was subsequently put to death. Winthrop makes no interpretive comment.[10]

In one particular adultery case, Winthrop attributes a woman's fall to her father's negligence. The father departed for England, leaving his daughters behind, "but took no course for their safe bestowing in his absence, as the care and wisdom of a father should have done" (*J*, 2:317). The cause is clear: the result as Winthrop explains it is that a married man "was taken with [one of the daughters], and soliciting her chastity, obtained his desire." The daughter, Mary Martin, having "committed sin" with this man in the house, became pregnant, killed the child after its birth, was found out, and condemned to death. In Boston the law forbade anyone from living alone; this narrative stresses the importance of membership with a legitimate family and a pious community. According to the colonial tradition, individuals by themselves faced a much greater risk of transgressing than those who were tightly bound into the community through family. Winthrop's prose style in this instance is especially terse and unembellished. He relates "a very sad occasion" in a most objective manner, leaving the condemnation of the woman to God: "she behaved herself very penitently while she was in prison. . . . Yet all the comfort God would afford her, was only trust (as she said) in his mercy through Christ" (*J*, 2:317). Such incidents are indicative of the terrible pressures on colonists to "move humbly and watchfully" in the New England community. Winthrop's report demands attention by its subject matter and must have been intended to compel readers to avoid the sins that would lead to such dire consequences. At the same time, it seems arguable that Winthrop himself laments the transgression and the tragic deaths of both mother and child.

When misfortune befell the unrighteous, Winthrop had no qualms about entering the episode into his journal. Despite his firm belief in justification by grace not works, he seems to suggest (as Hutchinson was banished for pointing out) sanctification (an honest, humble, industrious life-style according to the laws of the Bible and the model of Jesus) can help to evidence grace. Although God is free to strike down any one at any time for reasons beyond the understanding of man, that same God is somehow more likely to strike down the ungodly. After relating the shooting death of a Captain Patrick and describing his various transgressions, for example, Winthrop wrote that his death "was the fruit of his wicked course and breach of covenant with his wife, with the church, and with that state who had called him and maintained him, and he found his death from that hand where he sought protection" (*J*, 2:154). About a man who dies crossing the Atlantic, Winthrop writes "one of the seamen died—a most profane fellow, and one who was very injurious to the passengers" (*J*, 1:44).

With relative ease Winthrop discovers justice and the divine plan in these obvious cases. In reporting misfortunes that befell the godly without apparent logical or discernible cause, however, Winthrop has little explanation to offer other than to admit that any such incident was a sad accident. Often a moral can be implied either by context or by the circumstances of the narrative itself. Such is the case in the story about the accidental shooting death of a five-year-old whose father left him alone in the house. In their care and wisdom, Winthrop implies, fathers should know better than to leave children unattended in a room or house in which loaded guns are accessible.

Within the larger history of New England, many of these stories have as a common theme Satan's repeated-but-thwarted attempts to ruin the colonies. Winthrop noted that the "devil would never cease to disturb our peace, and to raise up instruments one after another" (*J*,

1:285). Whether referring to public goings-on or to private incidents and misfortunes, Winthrop believed that readers should be aware of the devil's work. In 1645 he wrote about the purpose of his journal: "It may be of use to leave a memorial of some of the most material, that our posterity and others may behold the workings of Satan to ruin the colonies and churches of Christ in New England, and into what distempers a wise and godly people may fall in times of temptation; and when such have entertained some false and plausible principles, what deformed superstructures they will raise thereupon, and with what unreasonable obstinacy they will maintain them" (*J*, 2:240).

Given the prevalence and the thematic importance of the stories that make up a large portion of the journal, it seems perfectly fitting that Winthrop's final entries (and perhaps his last surviving writing) would be stories of a private nature. The final entry, for example, tells of the drowning of a child of five whose father had worked into the Sabbath (Saturday night). Winthrop concludes by vindicating the parent to a degree: "But the father, freely in the open congregation, did acknowledge it the righteous hand of God for his profaning his holy day against the check of his own conscience" (*J*, 2:355).

In the nineteen years that Winthrop kept his journal, Massachusetts Bay changed from a small trading company to an established, virtually self-sufficient colony, part of a united federation of colonies. During these years Winthrop was always either at or near the head of the political and religious decision-making bodies. This proximity encouraged him to write many tracts concerning governmental and ecclesiastical decisions for which there was no room in the journal. The next chapter investigates many of these other writings.

Chapter Seven
Cheerful Submission to Authority: Miscellaneous and Later Writings

Judges are Gods upon Earthe.

(Winthrop Papers, 4:476)

Although the journal history of New England that John Winthrop kept for almost twenty years is unquestionably his most significant contribution to American literature, it is by no means his only important work. As we have seen, he wrote a historically important sermon, a documentary history of the Hutchinson trial (published in 1644), and a record of his conversion experience (1637). Throughout his career, the governor also wrote several less well-known tracts concerning politics, theology, and the colony's relations with the Indians.

Miscellaneous Early Writings

For the political and legal writing Winthrop would be called upon to do in New England, he had an apprenticeship in his native country. While he worked as an attorney from 1627 to 1628, for example, he prepared several bills evidently for presentation before Parliament. As Robert C. Winthrop describes them, they "are wholly in his own handwriting, on large paper, with ample margins, and prepared as if for the consideration of a Legislative Committee."[1] In one of these tracts he described the reasons for preventing drunkenness, arguing against the "loathsome vice of Drunkennesse": "An Act for the preventing of drunkenness and of the great waste of corn."[2] His concern is that beer is brewed too strong and thus "an excessive wast of Barlye, which might be imployed to the great good of the poore, and good of the whole kingdom" (*WP,* 1:371–74). Winthrop records facts and figures to argue his case, concluding that this law, if passed, could enrich the kingdom by five million pounds a year. Contrary to the modern stereotypical notion of Puritans as teetotalers, Winthrop was not against drinking in itself; he favored beer as a wholesome drink, but abhorred it as an intoxicant.

The bill, which might have been presented to the House of Commons in 1627 or 1628, never became law, but it is representative of several such pieces Winthrop wrote during his tenure at the Court of Wards and Liveries. Another tract attributed to Winthrop and written near the same time is "An Acte to settle a Course in the Assessinge and Levienge of Common Charges in Townes and parishes" (*WP*, 1:418–19). The bill proposes to establish a law concerning taxation that would end dissension about rates and collections for common charges for such public benefits as maintaining soldiers, prisons, bridges, and churches. Winthrop recognized a need for such taxation, and he gained valuable experience in attempting to organize a fair and workable means of taxation. Such experience would serve him well in New England.

In addition to gaining ability as a framer of legal tracts, Winthrop prepared himself thoroughly for his command as governor of a holy commonwealth. In the late 1620s, he attended church services regularly and copied into a notebook brief outlines of each sermon. He kept track of the preachers, the texts, and the main points of the arguments.[3] Certainly this minute record helped to prepare the governor for the composition of his own lay-sermon aboard the *Arbella* in 1630.

Reformation without Separation

In an early New England document, Winthrop combined his two types of writing skills as he composed a tract on the reasons for reformation without separation: "Reasons to prove a necessitye of reformation from the Corruptions of Antechrist which hath defiled the Christian Churches, and yet without an absolute separation from them, as if they were no Churches of Christ" (1631). Winthrop probably composed the tract in response to Roger Williams's refusal to become temporary teacher at the Boston Church. (He was offered the position while John Wilson was in England trying to convince his wife to join him in New England.) Winthrop voices essentially the same sentiment in the *Humble Request*, insisting that the colonists were not separating from the Church of England; rather they were merely reforming it from within.

Although the manuscript exists only in a fragment, Winthrop's method and argument are clear.[4] As he argued in his tract on the reasons for settling in New England in the first place, he admits that the churches in England are corrupt, but he maintains that they are not unsalvageable: "the Corruption of a thinge dothe not nullifie a thinge so long as the thinge hathe a beinge in the same nature, that it had, when it was in the beste beinge: so is it with the particular Congregations" (*WP*, 3:13). Referring to the Gospel of Matthew, Winthrop reminds his readers that the Bible prophesies that the visible church will stand until the end of the world. In response to the objection that the Church makes whores and drunkards of visible saints, he argues that "to terme the people in gen[era]l whores and drunkards is evill: for althoughe the most part are ignorant (the more is their sinne and our griefe) yet whores and drunkards they are not: weake Christians they are indeed, and the weaker for want of that tender Care, that should be had of them" (*WP*, 3:12). Because that church has become corrupt in England, transplanting, purifying, and caring for the visible church becomes the obligation and responsibility of the true Christians in New England. Winthrop thus takes a middle ground, arguing on the one hand that the Church of England needs reforming, while denying on the other hand that reformers have the right to separate from corrupt churches so long as they are "churches of Christ."

Defense of an Order of Court

Judging by surviving documents of Winthrop's writings, the Antinomian Controversy and the colony's troubles with Anne Hutchinson inspired one of Winthrop's greatest literary outpourings. In addition to the *Short Story* account, the journal entries, and his "Christian Experience," Winthrop wrote several tracts on different subjects related to the controversy. He engaged in a manuscript debate with Henry Vane concerning restrictions on immigration; he wrote a document concerning the power of the church; he also wrote arguments concerning works and grace, tracts which unfortunately do not survive.

Just after the proceedings against Wheelwright for his supposed sedition in March 1636, the General Court passed an order "to keep out all such persons as might be dangerous to the commonwealth" (*J*, 1:219). The order immediately followed Winthrop's election to the governorship after three years absence, and the reelected governor lost no time in publishing an explanation of the General Court's order.

In this explanation, Winthrop essentially argues that because the welfare of the whole should not be put at hazard for advantage of any individual, the magistrates of the commonwealth have the right to "receive or reject at their discretion." The document's full title is descriptive of its contents: "A Declaration of the Intent and Equitye of the Order made at the last Court, to this effect, that none should be received to inhabite within this Jurisdiction but such as should be allowed by some of the Magistrates" (*WP*, 3:423, 422).[5] Besides explaining the court's order, the "Declaration" is emblematic of Winthrop's view of the commonwealth. In phrases that are reminiscent of his "Modell of Christian Charity," the "Cambridge Agreement," and "Arguments for Plantation," Winthrop describes "the essentiall forme of a common weale or body politic" as he perceived it: "The consent of a certaine companie of people, to cohabite together, under one government for their mutual safety and welfare." Given this view of the commonwealth, Winthrop's argument is indicative of the sincerity of his intentions. He wanted what he felt was best for the colony: "The intent of the law is to preserve the wellfare of the body; and for this ende to have none received into any fellowship with it who are likely to disturbe the same and this intent (I am sure) is lawful and good" (*WP*, 3:422–23, 424).

Winthrop premises his argument on the political ideology current at the time, brought with the Puritans from Jacobean England, namely that "no man hath lawfull power over another, but by birth or consent." The commonwealth is founded by free consent of the members who "have a public and relative interest each in other." Echoing specifically the metaphor he expounds in the "Modell of Christian Charity" of 1630, Winthrop argues that every member of a commonwealth such as the one in New England is obligated "to seeke out and entertaine all means that may conduce to the wellfare of the bodye" (*WP*, 3:423). In the "Modell," we remember, he writes that "All the partes of this body being thus united are made soe contiguous in a speciall relation as they must needes partake of each others strength and infirmity, joy, and sorrowe, weale and woe" (*WP*, 2:289).

An objection that concerns the author of the defense is that the law may result in rejecting "good Christians and so consequently Christ himselfe" (*WP*, 3:425). The possibility of denying Christians a home in New England was a serious consideration for Winthrop, who earnestly desired and certainly recognized the need for immigration. He knew that not only religiously but also economically and politically the growth of the colony was imperative.

Because he sincerely believed that it would be wrong to deny a true Christian admittance into his holy commonwealth, Winthrop argues that the magistrates and elders have not yet, as far as they know, rejected a Christian. Moreover, he argues that rejecting the man would not necessarily be the same as rejecting Christ. Weak as it is, Winthrop's argument rests on that simple denial. He firmly believes that to admit those who threaten the peace and harmony of the commonwealth would be a sinful evil, and that he would be unfaithful to his duty as Puritan magistrate in receiving such. According to Perry Miller, Winthrop assumes "that man is a reasonable creature, and his statement of political theory in these papers owes more to logic than to the word of God."[6]

Because Henry Vane was not convinced by Winthrop's "Defense," he wrote an answer questioning both the author's logic and his authority as a magistrate. The young Henry Vane, who had recently been left out of the government altogether, was certainly bitter. As governor he had been the most important ally the Antinomians could have had. Unfortunately for Hutchinson, Wheelwright, and the others of their camp, his dethroning, as it were, cost them their stronghold in Boston, and ultimately their own rights to residence within the limits of the Bay Colony. In his response to Winthrop's "Defense," the ex-governor makes one last vain effort to confront his adversaries, an effort that is cogent and perhaps appealing to democratic ears.[7] Winthrop had written that "If we are bound to keepe off whatsoever appears to tend to our ruine or damage, then we may lawfully refuse to receive such whose dispositions suite not with ours and whose society (we know) will be hurtfull to us" (*WP,* 3:423). In response to this passage, Vane writes that "this kind of reasoning is very confused and fallacious . . . [the question is] whether persons may be rejected, or admitted, upon the illimited consent or dissent of magistrates."[8] According to Winthrop, Vane's answer cast "much reproach and slander . . . upon the Court." In other words, the General Court approved Winthrop's stance; and when the whole "proceedings about the law" was read before the court, most parties were satisfied, even "some that were on the adverse party, and had taken offense at the law, did openly acknowledge themselves fully satisfied" (*SS,* 251–52).

In his "Reply to an Answer Made to a Declaration," Winthrop essentially restates his former argument in the light of Vane's objections. (See *WP,* 3:463–76). The governor moves from point to point, methodically and patiently, showing in each case what his own argument is, what Vane's objection is, and how he refutes or answers Vane's objections. In this sense the "Reply" adds little new to the original "Defense." In other ways, however, the "Reply" is worthy of comment. Winthrop begins by condemning "Contentions among brethren . . . [as] sad spectacles (*WP*, 3:463). But because "the cause of truth and justice" calls to him, Winthrop feels obliged to respond even though he thereby continues the contention; he is careful to place the blame, however, on Vane: "if I deale more sharply, than mine owne disposition leads me, the blame must fall upon him, who puts such occasions upon me, as I cannot otherwise shunne" (*WP*, 3:463). Risking further contention, Winthrop verges on attacking the man rather than his argument, stating for example, that "his zeale for the cause outrunes his judgment" (*WP*, 3:468). In other instances Winthrop submits that Vane's argument is simply fallacious and does not merit a reply. Winthrop also accuses the addresser of merely babbling: "Thus he runs on in a frivolous discourse, and in the end falls upon this false conclusion" (*WP*, 3:465).

Whether or not Winthrop is guilty of an ad hominem argument, he was careful to avoid ever naming his adversary (although certainly the author of the "Address" was known to all who heard the tract read at court). Instead Winthrop designates him as the "Answerer," and generally refers to him with an anonymous third person pronoun. On occasion, however, Winthrop slips into the second person, under the pretense of a direct quote of a question Winthrop would ask him: "I must make bold to aske him this question, viz. Seeing you are bound by your oath" (*WP*, 3:472).

In justifying his position Winthrop emphasizes the duty of the magistrate. He states that the magistrates have made an oath both to the church and to the civil state, and that they also are under a sort of civil moral code that regulates their behavior: "As they are magistrates, they are sworne to doe right to all, and regulated by their relation to the people, to seeke their wellfare in all things" (*WP*, 3:466).

Winthrop felt that in the tight-knit, ideal holy commonwealth he advocated, such a system would be perfectly appropriate. The faith the members of a holy commonwealth needed to have in their magistrate would justify their belief in his righteousness. A magistrate was elected by the freemen, but once in office he was believed to have God's authority to perform his task. In a holy commonwealth, of course, the law of the Bible is the magistrate's guide, and the corruption of a magistrate, in this ideal circumstance, is out of the question. In setting up in Massachusetts the colonists agreed "to walke according to the rules of the gospell." In Winthrop's terms, one thus would have "a christian common weale."

According to the account in Winthrop's *Short Story,* the governor's reply to Vane's answer to the original defense was successful. Even some members of the opposing faction were convinced of the justice of the immigration law. Winthrop was successful here, as he would be again the next fall in banishing Wheelwright and Hutchinson. The established colony would survive the internal threats despite Satan's intention to distract or overthrow the churches in New England.

Former Passages

Besides the theological threats to the community, the colony was repeatedly beset with problems concerning the Indians, either as a result of the colonists' behavior toward them or the Indians' real or imagined threat to the Europeans' safety and welfare. In a seven-page pamphlet published by the commissioners for the United Colonies, *Declaration of Former Passages and Proceedings betwixt the English and the Narragansetts* (1645), Winthrop recounts the colonists' dealings with the Narragansett Indians between 1636, when a treaty was signed, and 1645, when the commissioners were armed and ready to fight. To a certain extent, the tract was a declaration of war.

Despite protestations to the contrary, much of the English interaction with the Indians involved deceit, subterfuge, and murder. Having badly defeated the Pequots during the wars of the 1630s, the colonists diminished their threat and even arranged a treaty with them. The colonists then turned to the Narragansetts, another powerful New England tribe. Miantonomoh, one of the most powerful of the tribe's chieftains, had come to the English—as the treaty between English and Narragansetts prescribed—to ask for permission to attack the Pequots in an effort to avenge an earlier attack by the Pequots. The authorities did not refuse permission, and in the battle that ensued Miantonomoh was taken prisoner. Although the colony's leaders had led Miantonomoh to believe he was an ally, they were suspicious of his trustworthiness and thought him too powerful for the good of the colonies.

While the commissioners were considering what action to take against the sachem, their ally Uncas of the Pequots reported that he had captured him, and loyally, "craved the commissioners advice how to proceed with him" (*DFP*, 2).[9] In a journal entry from August 1643, Winthrop describes the dilemma the commissioners had faced while they held Miantonomoh captive. Miantonomoh was rumored to have been the "head and contriver" of a conspiracy "to cut off all the English." He was also "of a turbulent and proud spirit"—just the type of man the Puritans would not tolerate. Fearing, therefore, that it would "not be safe to set him at liberty, neither had we sufficient ground for us to put him to death." The magistrates called upon the elders, letting them recommend that he be executed. Next the commissioners secretly informed Uncas that they had decided Miantonomoh should be put to death. Uncas obliged: "Onkus' brother, following after Miantunnomoh, clave his head with an hatchet, some English being present" (*J*, 2:135, 136).

The *Declaration* opens with Winthrop's reminder that the English "came into these parts of the world with desire to advance the kingdome of the Lord Jesus Christ and to injoye his precius Ordinances with peace" (*DFP*, 1). Despite these benevolent intentions on the part of the English, as Winthrop narrates it, the Indians were now forcing the settlers to war.

After narrating the circumstances surrounding Miantonomoh's murder—as if to justify the Bay Colony's action—Winthrop recounts the Indian's offenses against the state, dating back to 1637 when the chief signed a treaty and 1638 when he was reputed to have broken that treaty by attempting to murder Uncas and then actually killing a Pequot prisoner put in his charge. In relating Miantonomoh's execution Winthrop leaves out the details of the Indian's death. In fact, Winthrop describes it in the pamphlet in a jargon not unlike the political-military jargons of other ages: "Uncas hereupon slew an enemy, but not the enmity against him." Because of this surviving enmity, the troubles with the Narragansetts continued. After describing them, Winthrop was forced to conclude that the "premises being duly weighed it clearly appeares that God calles the colonies to a war." The governor concludes the declaration by insisting that Satan was again stirring up "many of his instruments against the Churches" (*DFP*, 4, 7).

As a defense of the English actions against the Indians, the *Declaration of Former Passages* stands in ironic contrast with the earlier writings about Indians in New England. The first ground of settling in Massachusetts, we remember, was for the propagation of the gospel to the Indians; the settlers would "come in with the good leave of the natives who finde benifight [benefit] allreaddy by our Neighbourhood" (*WP,* 2:141).[10] In contrast to this hopeful beginning, the *Declaration* asserts that military measures would have to be taken against the Narragansetts despite the colonists' former intention to bring them to the word of God. The ideal of delivering them from the snares of the Devil by converting them seems to have been forgotten.

Historian Francis Jennings calls the *Declaration* a "bill of charges against the Narragansetts, which was concocted, as usual, of a great many highly misleading words."[11] The most damning evidence is Winthrop's rendition of a letter Roger Williams sent, explaining that despite nearby troubles the Rhode Island Indians sought peace not war.[12] As Jennings demonstrates, the commissioners (Winthrop?) literally changed Williams's account to fit their need, which—according to the author—was to wage war against the Indians. This subterfuge by the colonists Jennings calls "mendacity extraordinary even among adepts."[13]

Other passages in the *Declaration* suggest Winthrop's attempt to mislead. He repeats, for example, phrases concerning the colonists' efforts to maintain peace even though the English have suffered "many injuries and insolencies" at the Indians' hands. Several times he refers to the Indians' violation of treaties. Meanwhile, according to Winthrop, the commissioners "in care of the publick peace, sought to quench the fire kindled amongst the Indians, these children of strife." The political nature of the *Declaration* is undeniable; Winthrop's method of twisting facts to suit his needs seems equally obvious. The tract shows Winthrop and his fellow commissioners at their manipulative, exploitative worst. As Jennings argues, this manipulation "shows a side of old John Winthrop's character that sorts badly with his reputation for integrity and gentleness."[14]

In the *Declaration,* as with so many of his writings, the governor demonstrates that he saw behind the trouble of the moment Satan working against the colony. Although we cannot forgive Winthrop and his fellow colonists for their mistreatment of the native Americans, we can view him in the context of his age.[15] We can acknowledge that his *Declaration* shows him to have had the perseverance necessary to build and maintain a city founded in and governed by the will of his God; to have had faith in the future of a holy commonwealth; and to have felt that the Indians, like the Antinomians, were threats to that future.

Defense of the Negative Vote

In addition to writing about the internal theological threats and the external military threats to the community, Winthrop repeatedly wrote about domestic political adversity, introducing, defending, or justifying his positions concerning various governmental regulations. The policy of a negative vote (right to veto) essentially divided the General Court into two groups, giving the magistrates the power to dissent from or override the other group's decision despite the magistrates' numerical minority. As such, the policy marks the beginning of bicameral government in the United States. The occasion for Winthrop's written defense of the theory of the negative vote in 1643 has a fascinating background.

Winthrop introduced the idea of negative vote shortly after he was succeeded in the governor's spot by Dudley in 1634. Winthrop had granted power to the deputies as they demanded as early as 1634, but he wished to maintain the magistrates' authority and power. As we have seen, the deputies were elected by the freemen of the Massachusetts Bay Colony. Each township sent representatives to be a part of the General Court. Magistrates were also elected by popular vote, but Winthrop saw a distinction between the two groups. The deputies were simply intended to be representatives of the people; magistrates, once elected, had the power of divine sanction. The deputies, however, outnumbered the magistrates and therefore had the potential to carry any vote, a fact that gave them great political power. A simple majority, of deputies and magistrates, would give deputies an advantage Winthrop did not believe they deserved. So he established the principle of the negative vote: "No Lawe etc: shall passe, as an Acte of the Court, without the Consent of the greater parte of the magistr[ate]s of the one parte, and the greater number of the Dep[u]tyes on the other parte" (*WP,* 4:386). Thus neither group, deputies nor magistrates, could pass laws or make judgments in legal cases without procuring a favorable majority from the other group. In this way Winthrop avoided what he called a "mere democracy," something abominable according to Winthrop's seventeenth-century outlook.

The law as Winthrop framed it remained silently on the books, as it were, until a legal battle about ten years after its inception brought it again to the forefront. The legal battle, Sherman vs. Keayne, arose over the rightful ownership of a pig. The General Court addressed the issue in June 1642, but the actual sow business, "a great business upon a very small occasion" (*J*, 2:64) began in 1636 when Captain Robert Keayne received a stray sow and evidently advertised it.[16] After a year he claimed to kill his own sow, retaining the stray. At this point Mrs. Sherman came forward, arguing that Keayne took her sow, but because he had killed it she could not identify it. The court decided in Keayne's favor, giving him three pounds for costs and twenty for damages. Mrs. Sherman with the help of George Story gained popular support, and got a witness "to confess . . . that he had forsworn himself." The case was reopened. The deputies tended to side with Sherman, and the magistrates with Keayne so that, as Winthrop writes in his journal, since the deputies far outnumber the magistrates (thirty to nine), "no sentence could by law pass without the greater number of both." The deadlock occasioned the popular party's, the deputies', denigrating the principle of the negative vote, asserting that it "had hindered the course of justice" (*J*, 2:64, 65, 66).

In a journal entry for June 1643, Winthrop explains the occasion for his writing "a small treatise" on the negative vote, "wherein he laid down the original of it from the patent, and the establishing of it by order of the general court in 1634, showing thereby how it was fundamental to our government, which, if it were taken away, would be a mere democracy." To this treatise "one of the magistrates as was conceived" made an answer, "undertaking to avoid all the arguments both from the patent and from the order" (*J*, 2:120). The surviving document is Winthrop's "Reply to the Answ[er] made to the Discourse about the Neg[ative] vote."[17]

In a style similar to the one he used in his reply to Vane's arguments about immigration laws, Winthrop states his case point by point. In his response he answers questions about the legality of the negative vote, and shows that it subscribes to the letter of the patent, is fundamental to Massachusetts Bay government, and is lawful and expedient. He also has something to say about "the proper place and power of the Dep[u]ties" (*WP*, 4:380).

In defending the negative vote Winthrop refers to the two documents most important to the commonwealth, the Bible and the Charter. Though his use of the Scripture in this instance is slight, he does refer to the Old Testament to point out that the negative vote saved Jeremiah "against the minde of the Preists" (*WP*, 4:389). Winthrop makes detailed reference to the Charter, arguing that the first question will be "best cleared by the Patent it selfe, wherein I will set down the very words themselves (so far as concernes the state of the

Question) and not leave out what may make against me, as the Answ[erer] often doth" (*WP*, 4:380). Winthrop uses the patent in two ways: one is to demonstrate that the negative vote is lawful according to the laws brought over from England initially; the other is to deprecate the answerer's method. In concluding his argument that the patent makes legitimate the negative vote, Winthrop becomes vehement: "I must Conclude, that either these words in our Patent doe give the magistrates a Neg[ative] vo[te] or els there was never any Neg[ative] vo[te] granted by any Patent or Comission by any kinge of England since Edw[ward] the 3ds time" (*WP*, 4:382).

Winthrop argues that the negative vote is fundamental to the commonwealth in that it marks a specific difference between one form of government and another. If the negative vote were taken away, Winthrop repeats, "our Government would be a meere Democratie" (*WP*, 4:382). As a seventeenth-century Puritan aristocrat, Winthrop had no sympathy with democracy. According to Winthrop, no precedent or warrant for a democracy existed in Scripture; "there was no such government in Israell." Correspondingly, for a new Israel in New England there should be none. Besides the lack of biblical precedent, secular histories record democracies as monsters, "the meanest and worst of all formes of Government," full of troubles, and short-lived (*WP*, 4:383). Democracy does not come highly recommended from Puritan New England. Ironically, of course, with the division of the General Court into two separate houses each with the power to veto, the modern bicameral aspect of government which is such an integral part of the democracy in the United States owes its genesis to Winthrop and Puritan New England.

Winthrop's mistrust of democracy lies in his doubts about the abilities of the common man to govern himself or others, a mistrust, incidentally, that was echoed by many of the framers of the Constitution some 150 years later. Winthrop did acknowledge that some deputies might boast accomplishments equal to those of a magistrate, but generally the magistrates were chosen specifically for their abilities in law and politics.

Finally, Winthrop addresses the objection that the negative vote gives undue power to the magistrates even if their judgment is unjust: "If the Court of Assist[ant]s should give an unjust sentence in any Cause, the partye injured can have no remedye in the generall Court if the magistr[ate]s (as they are like to doe) shall persist in their former

Judgment" (*WP,* 4:390). It is more likely, argues Winthrop, that the jury errs than the judge. Were judges to err, however, given new evidence that magistrates would "have good ground" to change their judgment. Magistrates are sure to be open-minded and "ready to attende such further helpe and light, as the wisdome and counsell of the generall Court may seasonably afforde." Furthermore, according to Winthrop, any unjust magistrate who persisted in error would be shamed into either correcting his error or leaving office.

We can only conclude that as Winthrop struggled to retain the power for the magistrates he had the benefit of the colony at heart. His ultimate motives may have been to some extent influenced by pride and human striving for fame, but regardless of what was personally best for the individual man, Winthrop sought what he thought and what the Bible taught was best for the commonwealth. Such thoughts guided him in devising and recording responses to the crises he and his colleagues faced.

Arbitrary Government

By midsummer 1643, Winthrop had satisfied, or at least quieted, the opposition concerning the negative vote. For a time he and the deputies "let the cause fall" (*J,* 2:121). By the following summer (1644) Winthrop had been voted out of the governorship; as deputy governor he opposed the deputies' claim of judicial authority, and he thereby caused them to accuse him of maintaining an arbitrary government. Once again Winthrop was put on the defensive.

To defend himself, the other magistrates, and the system of government in the Bay Colony, Winthrop again wrote a small treatise. Like his other titles, the full title of this treatise is descriptive: "Arbitrary Goverment described and the Common mistakes about the same (both in the true nature thereof, and in the representation of the Goverment of the Massachusetts, under such a notion) fully cleared" (1644).[18]

Winthrop's challenge in this treatise was to demonstrate that the government of the Massachusetts Bay Colony was not arbitrary. To this end he defines arbitrary government as that in which "a people have men sett over them without their choyce" who have power to govern them "without a Rule" (*WP,* 4:468). Where the people choose their own governors and require their own rules, in contrast, there is no arbitrary government. As he had done in defending the negative vote,

Winthrop referred directly to the Charter to show how the government of Massachusetts allows those liberties that keep it from being arbitrary.

A rhetorical trick Winthrop uses to his advantage is to define arbitrary government by negation and thereby imply the positive characteristics of the government he defends. The foundation, laws, and constant practice for the common good insist that Massachusetts offers liberties unknown to an arbitrary government. The foundation is in the Charter that prescribes the election of officers; the rules are established by the Charter, and the magistrates have been liberal in issuing punishment for transgressors of the rules. The rule observed by the magistrates is the word of God. Because of his divergence from the Bible in exacting penalties, Winthrop got in trouble with the deputies. He maintained that except for certain capital crimes, the punishment should vary with the circumstances of the crime. According to biblical precedent, argued Winthrop, penalties other than for capital offenses are not prescribed. The individual crime is considered in each case. Winthrop seeks to avoid oppressing the people by unjust sentences yet to punish adequately those who transgress against holy or civil law. Laws are objective and fixed; penalties subjective and relative.

In exacting punishments, Winthrop admits, a government can appear to be arbitrary. In a statement that anticipates the dictum "innocent until proven guilty," Winthrop writes that a human judge "cannot sentence another, before he hath offended, and the offence examined, proved, layd to the Rule, and weighed by all considerable Circumstances, and Libertye given to the partye to Answerer for himselfe" (*WP*, 4:474). By appealing to the accused's liberties, Winthrop argues that his government is not arbitrary, but liberal.

In contrast to this relatively liberal view, in perhaps the boldest statement he makes, Winthrop asserts that "Judges are Gods upon earthe." This statement verbalizes the seventeenth-century understanding of the judge's role in New England, but it also provides further evidence of Winthrop's naïveté, innocence, and hope. Again exhibiting his faith in the justice of Scripture and in the basic goodness of the magistrates in a holy commonwealth, Winthrop argues that the judges in their judgments will "holde forthe the wisdom and mercy of God" (*WP*, 4:476). God gives men the ability to interpret God's own laws.

Winthrop concludes by arguing that although laws should be fixed, firmly established, penalties should not be rigid. After all, in infinite wisdom, "God foresaw, that there would be corrupt Judges in Israell, yet he lefte most penaltyes, to their determination" (*WP,* 4:481). In answering objections, Winthrop acknowledges that judges are fallible, subject to temptation and error, but that the consequences of their error is slight compared with the injury an unjust law could do.

In the ideal commonwealth Winthrop envisions, knowing the laws will be sufficient cause for obeying them; the virtuous need not know the penalty. The best humans can do, submits Winthrop, is to provide against "common and probable events" (*WP,* 4:481). For the rest, the members of a holy commonwealth must trust in God.

The "Little Speech on Liberty"

No sooner had Winthrop argued that the government was not arbitrary than a group from the town of Hingham accused him of again overstepping his rightful authority. As with the sow business, here too a story stands behind Winthrop's creation of what has come to be known as his "little speech on liberty."[19] A group of townspeople from Hingham, a community near Boston, accused Winthrop of overstepping his authority when he appointed a militia captain contrary to the people's choice. The people of Hingham refused to respond to the appointed captain's orders and called Winthrop to court. Winthrop considered the Hingham faction mutinous and argued that he was honored in being singled out to defend a just cause. After being cleared of any criminal charges and reinstated, as it were, Winthrop "desired leave for a little speech" (*J,* 2:237). The speech he gave, as much as any other single piece of his writing, helps to characterize the man and to explain his theory of government.

After a short preface asking for the court's indulgence, Winthrop introduces the matters that his speech addresses: "The great questions that have troubled the country are about the authority of the magistrates and the liberty of the people." In his speech, then, he clarifies and expounds on the principle of authority and defines his notion of liberty. He acknowledges that even though he is a magistrate, he is also a person and, therefore, is subject to failings. Because he has been chosen by a godly people, however, he has his authority from God: "It is yourselves who have called us to this office, and being called by you, we have our authority from God." Yet unlike gods, magistrates come from among the electors, "men subject to like passions." Therefore, he cautions his audience, "when you see infirmities in us, you should reflect upon your own, and that would make you bear the more with us, and not be severe censurers of the failings of your magistrates, when you have continual experience of the like infirmities in yourselves and others" (*WP*, 4:238). If a judge's cases are clear, the magistrate—unless he "fail in faithfulness"—will be able to act appropriately. "But if the case be doubtful, or the rule doubtful, to men of such understanding and parts as your magistrates are, if your magistrates should err here, yourselves must bear it" (*J*, 2:238). In other words, Winthrop argues that unless a magistrate openly and obviously transgress the law of God, those who elect him must bear the consequences of his errors.

In discussing liberty, Winthrop again exhibits his belief in the ultimate goodness of God's covenanted people in the Bay Colony. He argues that there "is a twofold liberty, natural (I means as our nature is now corrupt) and civil or federal." He defines natural liberty as that of a brute beast, a liberty that has no place in a holy commonwealth: "By this, man, as he stands in relation to man simply, hath liberty to do what he lists; it is a liberty to evil as well as to good. This liberty is incompatible and inconsistent with authority, and cannot endure the least restraint of the most just authority" (*J*, 2:238). A "civil or federal, it may also be termed moral" liberty, in contrast, has "reference to the covenant between God and man. . . . This liberty is the proper end and object of authority, and cannot subsist without it. . . . This liberty is maintained and exercised in a way of subjection to authority." Such a liberty, argues Winthrop, is worth standing for with one's life. It is the liberty of being free and content to do God's will, to accept authority. Winthrop concludes by again contrasting natural and moral liberty: "If you stand for your natural corrupt liberties, and will do what is good in your own eyes, you will not endure the least weight of authority, but will murmur, and oppose, and be always striving to shake off that yoke; but if you will be satisfied to enjoy such civil and lawful liberties, such as Christ allows you, then will you quietly and cheerfully submit unto that authority which is set over you" (*J*, 2:238, 239). Winthrop's conception of liberty in this context epitomizes the belief of his age. Even though he was a judge, he also humbled himself in recognizing the interdependence of his fellow colonists. If he appeared happy in his harness, to paraphrase Robert Frost, it was only because he acknowledged that the success of the commonwealth depended on everyone being happy in harness. Winthrop's little speech delineates the accepted understanding of liberty in seventeenth-century Boston and is, if for no other reason, invaluable as a piece of literature.

Certainly Winthrop, like many of his colleagues in the government and the church, found his yoke "easy and sweet," yet some of the colonists did not. Those malcontents strove continually against the authorities. Much of Winthrop's writings in his journal and separate treatises attest to this continual struggle. Winthrop attempted to establish a holy commonwealth in which all members were parts of the same body, each dependent on the other, and he wrought a government suitable for the colony set on the edge of a vast wilderness continent.

Differences of opinion were inevitable. Jealousies and power struggles were a matter of course. Frustration and fear were the natural human responses to a community that was envisioned as an ideal holy commonwealth but discovered to be as real and as challengingly problematic as any community in the world. Winthrop's various literary responses to the many problems that beset him and his community in his career as governor of the Bay Colony demonstrate his ability to govern despite a multitude of problems, and make manifest—as historians have long recognized—that politically, socially, and religiously he was clearly the most able governor in Puritan New England. As his manifold writings attest, he must also be considered one of the most important American Puritan writers.

Chapter Eight
Legacy

that our posterity and others may behold the workings of Satan to
ruin the colonies and churches of Christ in New England.
(Winthrop's Journal, 2:240)

Near the entrance to the First Church of Boston at the corner of Berkeley and Marlborough streets stands a bronze statue of the community's
first governor. In his left arm he holds, not surprisingly, what must be
a Bible; and in his right hand he holds what may well be the Charter,
rolled into a scroll; the Bible he holds over his heart, the Charter
loosely by his side. The combination is appropriate: he holds the two
documents necessary to the well-being of his commonwealth. This
bronze reminder of the city's heritage symbolizes the principles by
which Winthrop governed the Bay Colony, and it also gives form to
the two principal sources for much of his writing, Bible and Charter.
The statue is emblematic of Winthrop's conviction that his writing
recorded the efforts of a chosen people in New England, a conviction
that informed much if not all of what he wrote in the New World. As
it evidences the importance Winthrop placed on the written word, the
statue also suggests the need he felt to make his own written record of
the history of the Massachusetts Bay Colony.

The importance of Winthrop as a literary figure cannot be denied,
especially when we consider that—with the exception of the works of
a few masterful poets—colonial American literature consisted almost
exclusively of histories, diaries, promotional tracts, sermons, and theological treatises. To ignore or fail to recognize these works is virtually
to negate or deny 150 years of American literature. Whether catego-
rized as history, religious philosophy, diary, or political tract, then,
Winthrop's body of writing has an important place in that history of
American literature.

Although virtually ignored as a literary artist, Winthrop has been
appreciated from the beginning as a historian. After his death in 1649,
many historians such as Mather, Hubbard, and Prince used his accounts in writing their own histories. Along with William Bradford's

Of Plymouth Plantation, Thomas Morton's *New English Canaan,* and Edward Johnson's *History of New-England, Winthrop's Journal* was one of the most significant contemporary histories available to later historians of New England. Despite Winthrop's preeminence as a historian, however, Robert Spiller and his coauthors in their *Literary History of the United States* acknowledge the governor's literary contribution only in passing: in comparison with Bradford, they conclude, "Winthrop's character was slightly more complex, and he did not always display the Christian charity of his contemporary at Plymouth. . . . They were [settling] a new country. . . . It was inevitable that they should want to write about what they were doing."[1] In another history of American literature, Marcus Cunliffe has little to say himself about Winthrop, but he does record a few disparaging remarks others have made about superstitious passages in Winthrop's journal.[2] The reputation of Winthrop's literary significance fares little better in the recent *Columbia Literary History of the United States.* Here, too, his history is compared unfavorably with Bradford's: "A mine of information, it quite lacks the integrity of Bradford's history, since Winthrop did not write retrospectively."[3] Given much less space than Bradford or Smith, Winthrop is nonetheless appropriately included among the masters of America's early chroniclers.

In his *History of Historical Writing in America,* J. Franklin Jameson briefly praises Winthrop's history as a narrative written by an impartial, informing, and thoughtful guide.[4] Michael Kraus concludes that "Winthrop's work sometimes reads like a newspaper which features sensational news rather than routine affairs: fires, shipwrecks, and sex scandals. On the other hand there was much which told of the creation of a society that built itself homes, schools, ships, and taverns. Scattered through it were the details, which when grouped together, told of the construction of a social organization more enduring than houses or ships or taverns."[5] Similarly, in David D. Van Tassel's *Recording America's Past,* Winthrop gets only one short paragraph.[6] Perhaps as interesting as these brief inclusions in several of the chronicles of colonial historians is his virtual or total exclusion from others. In a book on Puritan historians in America, for example, Peter Gay prefers Bradford to Winthrop as a representative seventeenth-century historian, devoting a full chapter to the Separatist yet barely mentioning Winthrop.[7]

In addition to this mixed response to Winthrop in literary and historical histories, many critics fault him for his Puritanism while applauding him for his account of early Massachusetts. An example of such a response is from the second editor of his journal. As explanation for why he cut the "repulsive details" of Hutchinson's miscarriage, Hosmer writes that they "are not inaccessible, and they only show how far bigotry could carry a mind naturally noble and magnanimous."[8] In the context of Winthrop's frequent entries concerning the special providences of God made manifest by occurrences in New England, Michael Kraus writes that in "Winthrop's *Journal* may be found an amusing example of the lengths to which an intelligent man would go in his will to believe."[9] What these historians and editors scoff at, ironically enough, is precisely that which represents one of the greatest values of Winthrop's work. Winthrop's strength and importance as a writer depends to a large extent precisely on those traits that characterize him as a Puritan, complete with what detractors call a Puritan's "bigotry" and "will to believe."

Even if with our "enlightened" late twentieth-century attitudes we fault Winthrop for the narrow-mindedness, intolerance, and superstition often associated with his Puritanism, we cannot fault him for his depiction of that Puritanism. As a historian Winthrop provides an invaluable account of his Puritan age. As a Puritan himself he exemplifies that age's beliefs as he records how those beliefs influenced and affected the building of the Massachusetts Bay Colony. Indeed, the very faults one finds in the man are evidence of the strengths of the author's written accounts. In one of intellectual history's sublime paradoxes, it is only by virtue of the authentic, deliberate, detailed historical account that critics know to find fault in the first place. Winthrop's obsession with misdirected sex or adultery, for instance, exemplifies the obsessions and concerns of the New England population in general. Winthrop's belief in the providence of God typifies the age's belief in God's providences. The sexism and racism evident in Winthrop's writings about Anne Hutchinson and the American Indians are vital characteristics of the age he describes.

This study has been designed in part to illustrate that Winthrop's life, the history of the colony, and his literary products are so interdependent, so interrelated, as to be inseparable if not indistinguishable. His history of New England is also his autobiography. In another sense, however, one can argue that there is a definite need to separate the man from his works. Only recently has anyone paid any attention to the literary merits or the conscious art of Winthrop's writing.[10] In 1984,

Everett Emerson wrote that Winthrop "has never been treated as a literary figure."[11]

Criticized for its lack of fluidity and its seemingly random juxtaposition of unrelated events, Winthrop's *Journal* is often unfavorably compared with Bradford's history. Yet some of the journal's very strengths are in these apparent faults. Kenneth Murdock praises Winthrop, writing that "All literature was for him a means to an end, and the most useful of all ends was, of course, to teach religious truth and to incite readers to follow God."[12] Often the juxtaposition of secular event and sacred meaning is so tight that the two become fused. In Winthrop's history we discover the settlers' belief that the Massachusetts Bay colonists were God's children, that providence worked in their favor, and that Satan (though ever-present) would ultimately be vanquished.

The opening passage of Winthrop's *Journal* demonstrates this fusion within a single entry: "Easter Monday.] Riding at the Cowes, near the Isle of Wight, in the *Arbella,* a ship of three hundred and fifty tons, whereof Capt. Peter Milborne was master . . ." (*J,* 1:23). Winthrop's entry concerns the strictly mundane, secular aspects of the ship. The entry includes mention of the wind, Mr. Cradock, the former governor, and the degree of readiness of the other ships. Yet this passage also refers to the specific day, "Easter Monday." Regardless of Winthrop's conscious reasons for so noting the day and date, the combination of the imminent departure and Easter indubitably confers on secular concerns the notions of a sacred new beginning, an ascension, a transformation from one life to another, a holy journey from an old world to a new. Such juxtapositions or fusions testify to the literary nature of Winthrop's historical record.

When he was forty-two, Winthrop left his patriarchal home in England, risked his established fortune, and forfeited the security of everything he had known in order to journey to the wilderness of New England. His journal and other tracts reveal that for nearly two decades he governed the infant colony, giving of himself, his fortune, and the last twenty years of his life. He came to build a city on a hill, a city that all eyes would be upon, to establish a holy commonwealth that would be a beacon for the rest of mankind. At the age of sixty-one, on 26 March 1649, John Winthrop died and was buried in Boston, the city he founded. He died a relatively poor but much respected man. As Nathaniel Hawthorne embellishes the story, a comet burned the letter *A* for angel through the sky the night of Winthrop's death: "as our good Governor Winthrop was made an angel this past night, it was doubtless held fit that there should be some notice thereof!"[13]

Nathaniel Hawthorne regarded not only Winthrop's death remarkable, he also found Winthrop's history of New England worthy of consideration. As Michael Colacurcio has recently argued, "Winthrop's famous *Journal* is not only a prime and obvious source of Hawthorne's knowledge of 'historical backgrounds' but . . . it furnishes the novel's [*The Scarlet Letter*] most essential themes. . . . Winthrop's record may itself be a vital part of Hawthorne's own (intensely historical) subject."[14] In addition to its importance to Hawthorne, Colacurcio argues for the history's merit in its own right. It is "an organized and vital history rather than a series of needful annals." A theme that unifies the entire document is "the sad and often exasperated feeling that a whole variety of misunderstandings about liberty are abroad in his land."[15] In its presentation of an age, then, Winthrop's writings have their own intrinsic merit; they are unquestionably valuable in their own right, but they also inform our generation of its own age as they informed other generations of their ages.

The literary value of Winthrop's work is not restricted to his journal. His speech on liberty captures the essence of a dominant Puritan attitude toward liberty and subjection to authority, an attitude that empowered the commonwealth's renowned first generation. His argument in "A Modell of Christian Charity" gives shape to the dream of the New World that the English colonists brought with them. In one complex passage in particular, for example, Winthrop personifies the body's need for the soul by comparing it to Adam's need for Eve: "shee [the soul] must have it [as Adam must have Eve] one with herself[;] this fleshe of my fleshe (saithe shee) and bone of my bone; shee conceives a great delighte in it, therefore shee desires nearenes and familiarity with it" (*WP*, 2:290–91). In its intricacy, the conceit vies for honors regardless of its author or origins.

Winthrop's description of the colonist's aspiration to build "a city on a hill" serves as the title for Loren Baritz's study of ideas and myths in America and is emblematic of his thesis that America's intellectual history owes its genesis, in part, to the combination of ordinary people and a magical, apparently limitless land. Winthrop's history is inordinately important, Baritz infers, in that in it he was recording the "cosmic climax of Boston's founding."[16]

Winthrop's life and writings provided Cotton Mather with the material to create a representative American biography. Sacvan Bercovitch studied this life to formulate his own notion of the Puritan origins of the American self.[17] In *The American Jeremiad,* Bercovitch uses as his point of departure Winthrop's "Modell of Christian Charity" to define a "rhetoric of mission" characteristic of the New England colonists. According to Bercovitch, Winthrop's sermon becomes a literature that defines and incorporates the literal and figurative promise of the New World.[18]

As these references suggest, modern America is greatly indebted to the body of literature Winthrop produced. It is as a writer that Winthrop the governor has been able to share with posterity his and his fellow colonists' hopes, dreams, and aspirations. He was able to preserve for future generations both the actual historical record of the building of Boston in New England and his vision of a city on a hill, not only as a model but as an emblem, a symbol of the potential of humanity: "wee must be knitt together in this worke as one man, wee must entertaine each other in brotherly Affection, wee must be willing to abridge our selves of our superfluities, for the supply of others necessities, wee must uphold a familiar Commerce together in all meekenes, gentlenes, patience and liberallity, wee must delight in eache other, make others Conditions our owne, rejoyce together, mourne together, labour, and suffer together, allwayes haveing before our eyes our Commission and Community in the worke" (*WP,* 2:294). Would that we as citizens of the world could be worthy of that respect and share that hope.

Notes and References

Chapter One

1. In *The Winthrop Family in America* (Boston: Massachusetts Historical Society, 1948), 3–10, Lawrence Shaw Mayo provides an account of John Winthrop's ancestors. See also Samuel Eliot Morison, *Builders of the Bay Colony* (Boston: Houghton Mifflin, 1958), 51–52.

2. Adam Winthrop's diary is found in the *Winthrop Papers,* 5 vols. (Boston: Massachusetts Historical Society, 1929–47), 1:39–144. Also important for a record of Winthrop's youth is Robert C. Winthrop's *Life and Letters of John Winthrop,* 2 vols. (Boston: Ticknor and Fields, 1864; reprint, New York: Da Capo Press, 1971). See also Edmund S. Morgan, *The Puritan Dilemma* (Boston: Little, Brown, 1958), 3–33; and Robert George Raymer, *John Winthrop: Governor of the Company of Massachusetts Bay in New England* (New York: Vantage Press, 1963).

3. Subsequent references to the *Winthrop Papers* (Boston: Massachusetts Historical Society, 1929–47) appear parenthetically in the text as *WP,* followed by volume and page numbers.

4. For this account of life at Cambridge, I am indebted to Samuel Eliot Morison, *The Founding of Harvard College* (Cambridge: Harvard University Press, 1935; reprint, 1968). See pages 60–78 for a description of the course of study for a degree at Cambridge in the early seventeenth century.

5. Morgan, *The Puritan Dilemma,* 6.

6. Morison, *Builders of the Bay Colony,* 54; R. C. Winthrop, *Life and Letters,* 1:59.

7. The *Winthrop Papers* (vol. 1, facing page 1) contains the Winthrop pedigree.

8. Alice Morse Earle's *Margaret Winthrop* (New York: Scribner's Sons, 1895; reprint, Williamstown, Mass.: Corner House, 1975) is the only book-length study of Winthrop's third wife. Joseph Hopkins Twichell, editor, has collected Margaret and John Winthrop's correspondence in *Some Old Puritan Love Letters—John and Margaret Winthrop—1618–1638* (New York: Dodd, Mead, 1893).

9. In *Puritanism in America, 1620–1750* (Boston: Twayne Publishers, 1977) Everett Emerson provides a succinct account of the Puritanism of John Winthrop's England. See also Patrick Collinson, *The Elizabethan Puritan Movement* (Berkeley and Los Angeles: University of California Press, 1967); Carl Bridenbaugh, *Vexed and Troubled Englishmen, 1590–1642* (New York: Oxford

University Press, 1968); and William Haller, *The Rise of Puritanism* (New York: Columbia University Press, 1938).

10. Perkins, "A Grain of Mustard Seed" (1597), in *The Work of William Perkins*, ed. Ian Breward (Appleford, England: Sutton Courtenay Press, 1970), 402, 396.

11. Perkins, "The Art of Prophesying," in *The Work of William Perkins*, 325.

12. See Edgar A. J. Johnson, "Economic Ideas of John Winthrop," *New England Quarterly* 3 (1930):235–50.

13. The text of the "Common Grevances" is printed in *Winthrop Papers*, 1:295–310.

14. George Robinson, ed., *John Winthrop as Attorney* (Cambridge: n.p., 1930) has collected and edited a volume of the extracts of the cases Winthrop handled as attorney. See also *Winthrop Papers*, 2:1–3, and Darrett Rutman, *John Winthrop's Decision for America* (Philadelphia: Lippincott, 1975), 20.

15. Charles Banks offers a detailed account of the voyage across the Atlantic in *The Winthrop Fleet of 1630* (Boston: Riverside Press, 1930).

16. On the organization of the new church-state system, see Morgan, *The Puritan Dilemma*, 84–100; and David D. Hall, *The Faithful Shepherd: A History of the New England Ministry in the Seventeenth Century* (Chapel Hill: University of North Carolina Press, 1972), 121–55.

17. See Everett Emerson, ed., *Letters from New England: The Massachusetts Bay Colony, 1629–1638* (Amherst: University of Massachusetts Press, 1976).

18. Subsequent references to *Winthrop's Journal: "A History of New England," 1630–1649*, ed. James Kendall Hosmer (New York: Scribner's, 1908; reprint, New York: Barnes & Noble, 1966), appear parenthetically in text as *J*, followed by volume and page numbers.

19. Edmund S. Morgan devotes a chapter to Winthrop's association with Roger Williams in *The Puritan Dilemma*, 115–33. See also Morgan's book-length study, *Roger Williams: The Church and the State* (New York: Harcourt, Brace and World, 1967). For an additional account of William's career in New England, see Perry Miller, *Roger Williams: His Contribution to the American Tradition* (New York: Atheneum, 1965).

20. See *Winthrop's Journal*, 2:100–5, for the text of *The Articles of Confederation Between the Plantations*.

21. "Israel Stoughton to John Stoughton," in *Letters from New England: The Massachusetts Bay Colony, 1629–1638*, 151.

Chapter Two

1. *The Works of Anne Bradstreet*, ed. Jeannine Hensley (Cambridge: Harvard University Press, Belknap Press, 1967), 240.

2. Robert Winthrop, *Life and Letters of John Winthrop*, 1:64.

3. The material gleaned from Robert C. Winthrop's *Life and Letters* is reprinted in *Winthrop Papers,* 1:161–69, 190–215, 235–38.

4. Robert C. Winthrop, *Life and Letters,* 1:66.

5. Richard Dunn, "Winthrop Writes His Journal," *William and Mary Quarterly* 41 (April 1984): 189, note 13.

6. Unless otherwise indicated, all references to "Experiencia" will be to volume 1 of the *Winthrop Papers* rather than to Robert C. Winthrop's *Life and Letters.*

7. Winthrop's various spellings of the word *secret* within a single sentence are indicative of the seventeenth-century's different rules governing spelling.

8. See Steven R. Smith, "Death, Dying, and the Elderly in Seventeenth-Century England," in *Aging and the Elderly: Humanistic Perspectives in Gerontology,* ed. Stuart F. Spicker, et al. (Atlantic Highlands, N.J.: Humanities Press, 1978), 216–17. See also David E. Stannard, *The Puritan Way of Death: A Study in Religion, Culture, and Social Change* (New York: Oxford University Press, 1977), and Gordon E. Geddes, *Welcome Joy: Death in Puritan New England* (Ann Arbor, Mich.: UMI Research Press, 1981).

9. See *Winthrop Papers,* 1:154, note 40.

10. John Owen King III finds it significant that Winthrop was about thirty years old when he underwent the conversion experience he narrated in his "Christian Experience"; see his *The Iron of Melancholy: Structures of Spiritual Conversion in America from the Puritan Conscience to Victorian Neurosis* (Middletown, Conn.: Wesleyan University Press, 1983), 58–60.

11. Robert C. Winthrop, *Life and Letters,* 1:78. For much of this analysis of Winthrop's "Christian Experience" I am indebted to both Daniel Shea's *Spiritual Autobiography in Early America* (Princeton: Princeton University Press, 1968) and Edmund Morgan's *Visible Saints: The History of a Puritan Idea* (New York: New York University Press, 1963).

12. For two recent discussions of the psychological effect on the believers of this doctrine, see Charles Cohen, *God's Caress: The Psychology of Puritan Religious Experience* (New York: Oxford University Press, 1986), especially chapter 2, "Covenant Psychology," 47–74; and David E. Stannard, "Death and Dying in Puritan New England," *American Historical Review* 78 (1973): 1305–30.

13. William Perkins, *Workes,* 3 vols. (London, 1608–31), 2:13. I am indebted to Edmund Morgan's description of Perkins's morphology of conversion. See *Visible Saints,* 67–69.

14. See Daniel Shea, *Spiritual Autobiography,* 89–90. See also John King, *The Iron of Melancholy;* and Patricia Caldwell, *The Puritan Conversion Narrative: The Beginnings of American Expressions* (New York: Cambridge University Press, 1983).

15. See Caldwell, *The Puritan Conversion Narrative,* 45–47.

16. Shea, *Spiritual Autobiography,* 106.

Chapter Three

1. Reference is to Cotton Mather's *Magnalia Christi Americana* (1702). In *Winthrop's Decision for America, 1629* (Philadelphia: Lippincott, 1975), 29–31, Darrett B. Rutman argues that Winthrop may have considered Ireland as a possible place of refuge, but not before the spring of 1629.

2. For this brief account of the history of the beginnings of the Massachusetts Bay Company, I am indebted to several sources. In addition to the documents reprinted in the *Winthrop Papers,* Thomas Hutchinson's *The History of the Colony and Province of Massachusetts-Bay* (Boston: Little and Brown, 1848; reprint, New York: Arno Press, 1972) is important. See also Frances Rose-Troup, *The Massachusetts Bay Company and Its Predecessors* (New York: Grafton Press, 1930; reprint, Clifton, N.J.: Augustum M. Kelley Publishers, 1973).

3. For a fuller discussion of the evolution of church polity and its relation to the civil state, see David D. Hall, *The Faithful Shepherd: A History of the New England Ministry in the Seventeenth Century* (Chapel Hill: University of North Carolina Press, 1972), 79–86. See also Perry Miller, *Orthodoxy in Massachusetts, 1630–1650* (Cambridge: Harvard University Press, 1933; reprint, Gloucester, Mass.: Peter Smith, 1965), esp. 148–211; Philip Gura, *A Glimpse of Sion's Glory* (Middletown, Conn.: Wesleyan University Press, 1984); and Richard Dunn, *Puritans and Yankees: The Winthrop Dynasty in New England, 1630–1717* (Princeton: Princeton University Press, 1962), 13–15.

4. Rutman, *John Winthrop's Decision for America,* 40.

5. In another context, Larzar Ziff discusses the reasons for emigration as evident from John Cotton's farewell address, "God's Promise to His Plantation"; see *The Career of John Cotton: Puritanism and the American Experience* (Princeton: Princeton University Press, 1962), 60–62. For a recent discussion of the reasons for the New England migration in the context of Winthrop's arguments, see Theodore Dwight Bozeman, *To Live Ancient Lives: The Primitivist Dimension in Puritanism* (Chapel Hill: University of North Carolina Press, 1988), 95–114.

6. For the details of composition and comparison of drafts see the editors' introduction and texts in *Winthrop Papers,* 2:106–51.

7. Rutman, *Winthrop's Decision,* 46; Stanley Gray, "The Political Thought of John Winthrop," *New England Quarterly* 3 (1930): 705.

8. Rutman, *Winthrop's Decision,* 46.

9. In this context Rutman suggests that Winthrop's son's misdeeds may have helped caused his disappointment with England and may have prompted him in his desire to leave (*Winthrop's Decision,* 24–25).

10. In *Changes in the Land: Indians, Colonists, and the Ecology of New England* (New York: Hill & Wang, 1983), William Cronon sets this Winthrop passage in context; see 56–57.

11. Miller, *Orthodoxy in Massachusetts,* 139.

12. On the details of the *Arbella* and rest of the fleet, see Charles Banks, *The Winthrop Fleet of 1630: An Account of the Vessels, the Voyage, the Passengers*

and Their English Homes from Original Authorities (Boston: Riverside Press, 1930), 33–34. See also Donald P. Wharton, "Anne Bradstreet and the *Arbella*," in *Critical Essays on Anne Bradstreet,* ed. Pattie Cowell and Ann Standford (Boston: G. K. Hall, 1983), 262–69.

13. Winthrop's lay-sermon has received much critical attention. Most recently, Edmund S. Morgan, in "John Winthrop's 'Modell of Christian Charity' in a Wider Context," *Huntington Library Quarterly* 50 (Spring 1987):41–64, argues that Winthrop's appeal for subjection to authority was a common motif among shipboard sermons of the time. In his book on the Puritan social ethic, Stephen Foster investigates the creativity in Winthrop's use of Christian doctrine; see *Their Solitary Way: The Puritan Social Ethic in the First Century of Settlement in New England* (New Haven: Yale University Press, 1971), 41–64. In addition to Loren Baritz, *City on a Hill: A History of Ideas and Myths in America* (New York: John Wiley & Sons, 1964), 14, see also Sacvan Bercovitch, *The American Jeremiad* (Madison: University of Wisconsin Press, 1978), 3–30; Stanley Gray, "The Political Thought of John Winthrop," *New England Quarterly* 3 (1930):681–705; Susan Power, *Before the Convention: Religion and the Founders* (Lanham, Md.: University Press of America, 1984), 65–73; and Darrett Rutman, *Winthrop's Boston: A Portrait of a Puritan Town, 1630–1649* (Chapel Hill: University of North Carolina Press, 1965), 3–22.

14. The best recent discussion on the structure of the Puritan sermon is Harry S. Stout, *The New England Soul: Preaching and Religious Culture in Colonial New England* (New York: Oxford University Press, 1986). See also Perry Miller, *The New England Mind: From Colony to Province* (Cambridge: Harvard University Press, 1953), 28–29. Perkins establishes the guidelines for the presentation of a Puritan sermon. See *The Works of William Perkins,* ed. Ian Breward (Appleford, England: Sutton Courtenay Press, 1970).

15. This excerpt is from the Geneva Bible (Geneva, 1560), reprinted in facsimile (Madison: University of Wisconsin Press, 1969).

16. See George Mosse, *The Holy Pretence: A Study in Christianity and Reasons of State from William Perkins to John Winthrop* (Oxford: Oxford University Press, 1957), 93–95.

17. Cotton, *Gods Promise to His Plantations* (London: William Jones, 1630), 14.

18. See Perry Miller, *Nature's Nation* (Cambridge: Harvard University Press, Belknap Press, 1967), 6–8.

19. See Bercovitch, *The American Jeremiad,* 3–30. For a reappraisal of the city-on-a-hill motif, see Bozeman, *To Live Ancient Lives,* 90–95.

Chapter Four

1. Morgan, *The Puritan Dilemma,* 134.

2. Several works address the Antinomian Controversy. In *The Puritan Dilemma,* for example, Morgan discusses Hutchinson in a chapter entitled "Seventeenth-Century Nihilism" but argues that Winthrop was "one of the

libelers" and writes that "Anne Hutchinson excelled him not only in nimble-
ness of wit but in the ability to extend a theological proposition into all its
ramifications" (134, 136). See also Selma R. Williams, *Divine Rebel: The Life
of Anne Marbury Hutchinson* (New York: Holt, Rinehart & Winston, 1981);
Emery Battis, *Saints and Sectaries: Anne Hutchinson and the Antinomian Controversy in the Massachusetts Bay Colony* (Chapel Hill: University of North Carolina
Press, 1962); and "Anne Hutchinson and the Antinomians," a chapter in
Philip Gura's *A Glimpse of Sion's Glory*, 237–75.

    3. See Williams, *Divine Rebel*, 63–76, for a detailed explanation of
possible reasons for the family's decision to settle in New England.

    4. Reference is to Winthrop's *A Short Story of the rise, reign, and ruine
of the Antinomians, Familists & libertines*, (London, 1644); reprinted in *The
Antinomian Controversy, 1636–1638: A Documentary History*, ed. David D. Hall
(Middletown, Conn.: Wesleyan University Press, 1968), 199–310. Subsequent references appear in the text as *SS*, followed by page number.

    5. See Williams, *Divine Rebel*, 73–74, 79–80.

    6. The account of the theological fine points of the Antinomian Con-
troversy presented in this chapter are necessarily brief. An indispensable account of the theological aspects of the controversy is William K. B. Stoever,
*"A Faire and Easie Way to Heaven": Covenant Theology and Antinomianism in Early
Massachusetts* (Middletown, Conn.: Wesleyan University Press, 1978). In the
context of Winthrop's journal entry, see pp. 9–10.

    7. John Wheelwright, "A Fast-Day Sermon" (Boston: 1637); reprinted
in *Antinomian Controversy*, 154.

    8. Ibid., 158.

    9. Ibid., 165, 166.

    10. See T. H. Breen, *The Character of the Good Ruler: A Study of Puritan
Political Ideas in New England, 1630–1730* (New Haven: Yale University
Press, 1970), 3–7.

    11. Gura, *A Glimpse of Sion's Glory*, 254–55.

    12. Morgan, *Puritan Dilemma*, 147–48; "Examination of Mrs. Hutch-
inson," in *Antinomian Controversy*, 311.

    13. Gura, *Glimpse of Sion's Glory*, 239.

    14. "Examination of Mrs. Hutchinson," *Antinomian Controversy*, 316.

    15. Ibid., 334.

    16. Compare Winthrop's *Short Story* (271) with the anonymous version,
"Examination of Mrs. Hutchinson," in *Antinomian Controversy*, 336–38 and
341.

    17. "Examination of Mrs. Hutchinson," in *Antinomian Controversy*, 343.

    18. Ibid., 348.

    19. For Winthrop's account of the trial, see *Antinomian Controversy*, 300–
10; for the anonymous report, see "A Report of the Trial of Mrs. Anne Hutchinson before the Church of Boston," in *Antinomian Controversy*, 349–88.

    20. See Battis, *Saints and Sectarians*, 233–35, for an explanation of
Hutchinson's newfound interest in death and resurrection.

21. "A Report of the Trial," in *Antinomian Controversy,* 388.

22. In the context of Mary Dyer's monstrous birth, of course, Winthrop has recorded Dyer's act of accompanying Hutchinson; see *Antinomian Controversy,* 281.

23. See Margaret Richardson and Arthur Hertig, "New England's First Recorded Hydatidiform Mole," *New England Journal of Medicine* 260 (1959):544–45. See also Anne Jacobson Schutte, "'Such Monstrous Births': A Neglected Aspect of the Antinomian Controversy," *Renaissance Quarterly* 38 (Spring 1985): 85–106.

Chapter Five

1. For the following account of the publication history of Winthrop's journals, I am indebted to Malcolm Freiberg, "The Winthrops and Their Papers," *Proceedings of the Massachusetts Historical Society* 80 (1968):55–70, and to Richard S. Dunn, "John Winthrop Writes His Journal," *William and Mary Quarterly* 41 (April 1984):186–88. See also Barbara McCrimmon, "John Winthrop's Journal," *Manuscripts* 24 (Spring 1972):87–96.

2. Dunn, "Winthrop Writes His Journal," 187.

3. *Winthrop's Journal,* 1:277, note 2.

4. Ibid., 2:46, note 1.

5. Hosmer's cuts occur on pages 1:277; 2:46, 55, 274. The missing material can be found in James Savage, *The History of New England* (Boston: Massachusetts Historical Society, 1853) as follows: 1:326, 327–28; 2:54–60, 76, 324.

6. See *Winthrop Papers,* 2:260. On the manuscript page beginning with Wednesday, 9 June 1630, Winthrop describes a small rock, and on the opposite page he draws a rough outline of the coast of Maine. Savage refers to the map; see *The History of New England* (1825), 1:29, note 2. A microfilm copy of the autograph notebooks is available from the Massachusetts Historical Society, *Winthrop Family Papers, 1537–1905,* reel 35.

7. The obviously much needed and more definitive edition of Winthrop's journals is promised by Laetitia Yeandle and Richard S. Dunn. See Dunn, "Winthrop Writes His Journal," 188.

8. Dunn, "Winthrop Writes His Journal," 185.

9. Compare *Winthrop's Journal,* 1:163.

10. Compare, ibid., 1:166.

11. See ibid., 1:96–97.

12. Winthrop and his Puritan contemporaries preferred using numerals to identify the months, thereby avoiding names derived from the Roman or pagan gods. I refer to the months by name for the sake of convenience.

13. Compare *Winthrop's Journal,* 1:119.

14. This particular text corresponds to *Winthrop's Journal,* 1:119.

15. Dunn, "Winthrop Writes His Journal," 206–7.

16. Ibid., 192.

17. Ibid., 207.

18. Yeandle and Dunn have evidently decided to call their forthcoming edition *The Journal of John Winthrop, 1630–1649, ibid.*, 188.

19. The best modern account of the building of Boston is Rutman, *Winthrop's Boston: A Portrait of a Puritan Town, 1630–1649.*

20. See, for example, David Levin, "William Bradford," in *Major Writers of Early American Literature,* ed. Everett Emerson (Madison: University of Wisconsin Press, 1972), 25–31.

21. See Morgan, *The Puritan Dilemma,* 59–61.

22. Ibid., 104.

23. For the various accounts of Williams's career, see chapter 1, note 19.

24. For Winthrop's account see *Winthrop's Journal,* 1:57, 116–17, 142, 149, 154, 162, 168.

25. See Morgan, *Puritan Dilemma,* for the text of the letter, 129.

26. See *Winthrop Papers,* vol. 3, for Williams's correspondence with Winthrop.

27. For brief discussion of the psychology of European response to the Indians, see Richard Slotkin, *Regeneration through Violence: The Mythology of the American Frontier, 1600–1860* (Middletown, Conn.: Wesleyan University Press, 1973), 25–56. Several historians have used Winthrop's journal in their interpretations of Anglo-American war with the Indians. See, for example, Alden T. Vaughan, *New England Frontier: Puritans and Indians, 1620–1675* (1965); rev. ed., New York: Norton, 1979), and Francis Jennings, *The Invasion of America: Indians, Colonialism, and the Cant of Conquest* (Chapel Hill: University of North Carolina Press, 1975).

28. For Winthrop's account of the Pequot War, see *Winthrop's Journal,* 1:118–40.

29. Alden T. Vaughan, *New England Frontier,* 122–54, discusses the Pequot War. See also Francis Jennings, *The Invasion of America,* 178–79, 187–201.

30. For a discussion of The English view of the American "savage," see Francis Jennings, *The Invasion of America,* 58–84.

31. *Winthrop's Journal,* 2:105–6.

32. Ibid., 2:108, note 1.

33. Philip Gura offers a detailed examination of Gorton's involvement with Massachusetts Bay; see *A Glimpse of Sion's Glory,* 276–303. See also Robert Emmet Wall, Jr., *Massachusetts Bay: The Crucial Decade, 1640–1650* (New Haven: Yale University Press, 1972), 121–56.

34. Morgan discusses the granting of the rights in the 1630 meetings, *Puritan Dilemma,* 89–92. See also *Massachusetts Colonial Records,* 23 August 1630. Concerning the Child affair, see Wall, *Crucial Decade,* 157–233.

35. Winthrop's account of the Child affair is found in *Winthrop's Journal,* 2:271–72, 289–317, 339–41.

Chapter Six

1. Dunn's work on Winthrop and his journal is extensive. See "Experiments Holy and Unholy, 1630–31," in K. R. Andrews et al., *The Westward Enterprise: English Activities in Ireland, the Atlantic, and America, 1480–1650* (Detroit: Wayne State University Press, 1979), 271–89. See also "Seventeenth-Century English Historians of America," in James Morton Smith, ed., *Seventeenth-Century America: Essays in Colonial History* (Chapel Hill: University of North Carolina Press, 1959), 195–225. Most recently Dunn has elaborated on the composition of the journal in "John Winthrop Writes His Journal," 185–212.

2. McCrimmon, "John Winthrop's Journal," *Manuscripts,* 24, 2 (1972):87–96.

3. Power, *Before the Convention: Religion and the Founders,* 65–106.

4. Miller, *The New England Mind: The Seventeenth Century* (New York: Macmillan, 1939; reprint, Cambridge: Harvard University Press, 1954), 360.

5. See Charles E. Banks, *The Winthrop Fleet of 1630,* 33–45. In a letter dated 14 August 1630 Winthrop mentions a chart of the sea voyage that Peter Milbourne, captain of the *Arbella,* drew for him (see *Winthrop Papers,* 2:309).

6. The best modern edition of Higginson's "True Relation" is in *Letters from New England: The Massachusetts Bay Colony, 1629–1638,* ed. Everett Emerson, 12–24. It is also reprinted in Hutchinson's *Collection of Original Papers* (Boston: Prince Society Publications), 32–47, and in *Chronicles of the First Planters of the Colony of Massachusetts Bay, 1623–1636,* ed. Alexander Young (Boston: 1846), 215–238, 260–64. See *Winthrop Papers,* 2:157, for the letter in which Winthrop mentions Higginson's "booke." See also Dunn, "Winthrop Writes His Journal," 190–91.

7. It is interesting to note that Winthrop's model, the Higginson account, also gives much space to descriptions of the wind (see Emerson, ed., *Letters,* 12–24).

8. Unless otherwise noted, subsequent references to Winthrop's journal, in this chapter are to Hosmer, ed., *Winthrop's Journal.*

9. *History of New England,* ed. James Savage (1825), 1:271. Hosmer felt obliged to omit Winthrop's account of the "monstrous birth" (*J,* 1:277, note 2). For the text of Winthrop's account, see the Savage edition, 1:271–73.

10. This is another of the several passages Hosmer decided not to include in his edition of the journal. See *The History of New England,* ed. Savage (1825), 2:61.

Chapter Seven

1. Robert C. Winthrop, *Life and Letters of John Winthrop,* 1:221.

2. In this context, *corn* is meant in the British sense of grain in general, and specifically, as Winthrop makes clear in the paper, barley.

3. See Robert C. Winthrop, *Life and Letters,* 1:262. The autograph volume of these sermon notes is housed in the Massachusetts Historical Society. A microfilm reprint is available in the *Winthrop Family Papers, 1537–1905,* reel 35.

4. The fragment is reprinted in *Winthrop Papers,* 3:10–14.

5. For the text of the "Declaration," see *Winthrop Papers,* 3:422–26.

6. Perry Miller, *Errand into the Wilderness* (Cambridge: Harvard University Press, 1956), 70.

7. Winthrop summarizes the debate in his *Short Story.* See *Antinomian Controversy,* ed. Hall, 251.

8. For Vane's answer to Winthrop's defense, see Thomas Hutchinson, *Collection of Original Papers Relative to the History of Massachusetts Bay* (Boston: Prince Society Publication, 1865), 1:74 and following.

9. Subsequent references to Winthrop's *A Declaration of Former Passages Betwixt the English and the Narrowgansets* (Boston: By Order of the Commissioners for the United Colonies, 1645) appear in the text as *DFP* and page.

10. Judging by historical evidence, one cannot be too sure of the Puritan settlers' sincerity concerning the conversion of the Indians. Besides the work of John Eliot, little was done to introduce the word of God to the native Americans. See Francis Jennings, *The Invasion of America,* especially 228–53.

11. Jennings, *The Invasion of America,* 274.

12. The text of Roger Williams's letter is reprinted in *Winthrop Papers,* 4:30–31.

13. Jennings, *Invasion,* 275.

14. Ibid., 274.

15. In his biting appraisal, Jennings is not nearly so generous. See Jennings, *Invasion,* 265–76.

16. For Winthrop's account of the episode, see *Winthrop's Journal,* 2:116.

17. See *Winthrop Papers,* 4:380–91, for the text of Winthrop's "Reply to the Answ[er]."

18. For the text of Winthrop's "Arbitrary Government," see *Winthrop Papers,* 4:468–88.

19. For Winthrop's account of events leading up to his writing of the little speech and for the text of the speech itself, see his *Journal,* 2:229–40.

Chapter Eight

1. Robert E. Spiller et al., *Literary History of the United States* (New York: Macmillan, 1946; rev. ed., 1960), 34.

2. See Marcus Cunliffe, *The Literature of the United States* (New York: Pelican Books, 1954; reprint, New York: Viking Penguin, 1986), 31.

3. Everett Emerson, "History and Chronicle," in *Columbia Literary History of the United States,* ed. Emory Elliott (New York: Columbia University Press, 1988), 50.

4. J. Franklin Jameson, *The History of Historical Writing in America* (Boston: Houghton Mifflin, 1891; reprint, Dubuque, Iowa: William C. Brown Reprint Library, 1962), 21–29.

5. Michael Kraus, *The Writing of American History* (Norman: University of Oklahoma Press, 1953), 26–27. In his earlier *A History of American History* (New York: Farrar & Rinehart, 1937), 39–45, is found a similar critique of Winthrop as historian.

6. David D. Van Tassel, *Recording America's Past: An Interpretation of the Development of Historical Studies in America, 1607–1884* (Chicago: University of Chicago Press, 1960), 13–14.

7. Peter Gay, *A Loss of Mastery: Puritan Historians in Colonial America* (Berkeley and Los Angeles: University of California Press, 1966). In addition to Bradford, Gay considers Cotton Mather and Jonathan Edwards.

8. *Winthrop's Journal*, 1:277, note 2.

9. Kraus, *A History of American History*, 43.

10. Helpful in the context of the significance of Puritan history is David Levin's "William Bradford: The Value of Puritan Historiography," in *Major Writers of Early American Literature,* ed. Everett Emerson (Madison: University of Wisconsin Press, 1972), 11–31.

11. Everett Emerson, "John Winthrop," in *Dictionary of Literary Biography,* vol. 24, *American Colonial Writers, 1606–1734,* ed. Emory Eliot (Detroit: Gale Research Company, 1984), 359.

12. Kenneth Murdock, *Literature and Theology in Colonial New England* (Cambridge: Harvard University Press, 1949), 96–97.

13. Nathaniel Hawthorne, *The Scarlet Letter* (1850; reprint, Columbus: Ohio State University Press, 1962), 158.

14. Michael J. Colacurcio, "'The Woman's Own Choice': Sex, Metaphor, and the Puritan 'Sources' of *The Scarlet Letter,*" in *New Essays on "The Scarlet Letter"* (Cambridge: Cambridge University Press, 1985), 103.

15. Ibid., 106, 107.

16. Baritz, *City on a Hill: A History of Ideas and Myths in America,* 31.

17. See Sacvan Bercovitch, *The Puritan Origins of the American Self* (New Haven: Yale University Press, 1975).

18. Bercovitch, *The American Jeremiad,* 8.

Selected Bibliography

PRIMARY WORKS

Published Works

Works by John Winthrop are arranged alphabetically by title. Many of the titles referred to throughout this study are available in the *Winthrop Papers*. In addition to the first title cited, other editions or publications of works are noted within each citation as appropriate.

Antinomians and Familists Condemned by the synod of Elders in New-England: with the proceedings of the magistrates against them, and their apology for the same. . . . London: Printed for R. Smith, 1644. Republished as *A Short Story of the rise, reign, and ruin of the Antinomians, Familists & libertines. . . .* London: Printed for Ralph Smith, 1644. Reprinted in *The Antinomian Controversy, 1636–1638: A Documentary History,* 199–310. Edited by David D. Hall. Middletown, Conn.: Wesleyan University Press, 1968.

A Declaration of Former Passages and Proceedings Betwixt the English and the Narrowgansets, with Their Confederates, Wherein the Grounds and Justice of the Ensuing Warre Are Opened and Cleared. Boston: Commissioners for the United Colonies, 1645.

John Winthrop as Attorney: Extracts from the Order Books of the Court of Wards and Liveries, 1627–1629. Edited by George W. Robinson. Cambridge: n.p., 1930.

A Journal of the Transactions and Occurrences in the Settlement of Massachusetts and the Other New-England Colonies, from the Year 1630 to 1644. Edited by Noah Webster. Hartford: Printed by Elisha Babcock, 1790. Reedited and published as *The History of New England from 1630 to 1649.* 2 vols. Edited by James Savage. Vol. 1, Boston: Phelps and Farnham, 1825; vol. 2, Boston: T. B. Wait and Son, 1826. Revised edition, Boston: Little, Brown, 1853. Republished as *Winthrop's Journal "History of New England," 1630–1649.* 2 vols. Edited by James Kendall Hosmer. New York: Scribner's Sons, 1908. Reprint. New York: Barnes and Noble, 1966.

Some Old Puritan Love-Letters—John and Margaret Winthrop—1618–1638. Edited by Joseph Hopkins Twichell. New York: Dodd, Mead, 1893.

Winthrop Family Papers, 1537–1905. Boston: Massachusetts Historical Society. Microfilm, 53 reels.

Winthrop Papers. 5 vols. Boston: Massachusetts Historical Society, 1929–47.

Manuscripts

Winthrop's manuscripts are housed in the archives of the Massachusetts Historical Society. Besides the microfilm version of the manuscripts, most of Winthrop's papers have been printed.

"Notes on Sermons Heard by John Winthrop on Sundays and Prayer Days During a Large Part of the Years 1627 and 1628."
"Stile's, 'Excerpta.'" Belknap MS. 161.A. Vol. 1. 167–68. Boston: Massachusetts Historical Society.

SECONDARY WORKS

Of the scores of books written about the governor and the first two decades of the Massachusetts Bay Colony, the following seem exceptionally important in the context of John Winthrop. Additional books and articles are cited in the notes.

Books and Parts of Books

Banks, Charles E. *The Winthrop Fleet of 1630: An Account of the Vessels, the Voyage, the Passengers and Their English Homes from Original Authorities*. Boston: Riverside Press, 1930. Detailed account of Winthrop's transatlantic voyage.
Baritz, Loren. *City on a Hill: A History of Ideas and Myths in America*. New York: John Wiley & Sons, 1964. First chapter devoted to political theology of John Winthrop.
Bercovitch, Sacvan. *The Puritan Origins of the American Self*. New Haven: Yale University Press, 1975. Refers to Cotton Mather's biography of Winthrop to establish characteristics of representative American biography.
————. *The American Jeremiad*. Madison: University of Wisconsin Press, 1978. Uses Winthrop's "Modell" as prototext upon which to base argument for jeremiad as influential American genre.
Caldwell, Patricia. *The Puritan Conversion Narrative: The Beginnings of American Expression*. New York: Cambridge University Press, 1983. Includes an important chapter on the morphology of conversion.
Cowell, Henry J. *John Winthrop: A Seventeenth Century Puritan Romance*. Colchester, England: Benham and Company, 1949. Presents favorable account of Winthrop as statesman.
Dunn, Richard S. *Puritans and Yankees: The Winthrop Dynasty of New England, 1630–1717*. Princeton: Princeton University Press, 1962. First two

chapters consider Winthrop's role as governor in the context of New England history.

Emerson, Everett. *"John Winthrop."* In *American Colonial Writers, 1606–1734*, ed. Emory Elliott, vol. 24 of *Dictionary of Literary Biography*. Detroit: Gale Research Company, 1984. Succinct account of Winthrop's life and major writings.

————, ed. *Letters from New England: The Massachusetts Bay Colony, 1629–1638.* Amherst: University of Massachusetts Press, 1976. History of first ten years of Bay Colony as told through letters by the founders, including twenty-one letters by Winthrop.

Gura, Philip F. *A Glimpse of Sion's Glory: Puritan Radicalism in New England, 1620–1660.* Middletown, Conn.: Wesleyan University Press, 1984. Argues that New England colonists had great variety of theological opinion.

MacPhail, Andrew. *Essays in Puritanism.* London: T. Fisher Urwin, 1905. Devotes chapter to political biography of Winthrop.

McWilliams, Wilson Carey. *The Idea of Fraternity in America.* Berkeley and Los Angeles: University of California Press, 1973. One chapter devoted to Winthrop's political and social theories.

Mather, Cotton. *Magnalia Christi Americana.* London, 1702. Includes an eulogistic chapter on the life of Winthrop.

Mayo, Lawrence Shaw. *The Winthrop Family in America.* Boston: Massachusetts Historical Society, 1948. Biographical account of Winthrop.

Miller, Perry. *Orthodoxy in Massachusetts, 1630–1650.* Cambridge: Harvard University Press, 1933. Reprint, Gloucester, Mass.: Peter Smith, 1965. Provides important theological background for Puritan New England.

Morgan, Edmund S. *The Puritan Dilemma: The Story of John Winthrop.* Boston: Little, Brown, 1958. Remains a fine biographical account of Winthrop and history of Massachusetts Bay.

————. *Visible Saints: The History of a Puritan Idea.* New York: New York University Press, 1963. Provides important background material for New England Puritanism.

Morison, Samuel Eliot. *Builders of the Bay Colony.* Boston: Houghton Mifflin, 1930. Reprint, 1958. In a chapter devoted to Winthrop, discusses several of Winthrop's works in historical context.

Mosse, George L. *The Holy Pretence: A Study in Christianity and Reason of State from William Perkins to John Winthrop.* Oxford: Basil Blackwell, 1957. Reprint, New York: Howard Fertig, 1968. Provides valuable analysis of "Modell of Christian Charity."

Noble, John and John F. Cronin, eds. *Records of the Court of Assistants of the Colony of the Massachusetts Bay, 1630–1692.* 3 vols. Boston: Published by the County of Suffolk, 1901–28. Provides contemporary accounts of the General Court.

Power, M. Susan. *Before the Convention: Religion and the Founders.* Lanham,

Md.: University Press of America, 1984. Compares Winthrop's writings with those of other early American political philosophers.

Raymer, Robert George. *John Winthrop: Governor of the Company of Massachusetts Bay in New England.* New York: Vantage Press, 1963. Biography of Winthrop.

Rose-Troup, Frances (James). *The Massachusetts Bay Company and Its Predecessors.* New York: Graften Press, 1930. Reprint, Clifton, N.J.: Augustus M. Kelley Publishers, 1973. Still valuable historical account of the founding of the Bay Colony.

Rutman, Darrett B. *John Winthrop's Decision for America: 1629.* Edited by Harold M. Hyman. Philadelphia: J. B. Lippincott, 1975. Detailed account of Winthrop's decision to emigrate; includes relevant primary documents.

————. *Winthrop's Boston: Portrait of a Puritan Town, 1630–1649.* Chapel Hill: University of North Carolina Press, 1965. Superb account of the Boston Winthrop founded and lived in; includes critiques of several of Winthrop's works.

Shea, Daniel B., Jr. *Spiritual Autobiography in Early America.* Princeton: Princeton University Press, 1968. Discusses Winthrop's "Christian Experience" in context of traditional Puritan spiritual narratives.

Shurtleff, Nathaniel B., ed. *Records of the Governor and Company of the Massachusetts Bay in New England.* 6 vols. Boston: Printed by Order of the Legislature, 1853–54. Provides contemporary accounts of Winthrop's government.

Winthrop, Robert C. *Life and Letters of John Winthrop.* 2 vols. Boston: Ticknor & Fields, 1864, 1867. Reprint, New York: Da Capo Press, 1971. First complete and still valuable biography of Winthrop; includes a great deal of primary material.

Ziff, Larzer. *The Career of John Cotton: Puritanism and the American Experience.* Princeton: Princeton University Press, 1962. Excellent account of Bay Colony with focus on colony's most important minister.

Articles

Dunn, Richard S. "Experiments Holy and Unholy, 1630–1." In *The Westward Enterprise: English Activities in Ireland, the Atlantic, and America, 1480–1650,* edited by K. R. Andrews et al, 271–89. Detroit: Wayne State University Press, 1979. Compares Winthrop's with Henry Colt's sea journal.

————. "John Winthrop Writes His Journal." *William and Mary Quarterly* 41 (April 1984):185–212. Superb account of Winthrop and the composition of his journal.

Gray, Stanley. "The Political Thought of John Winthrop." *New England Quarterly* 3 (1930): 681–705. Bases critique of Winthrop's political thought on opening of "Modell of Christian Charity."

Johnson, Edgar A. J. "Economic Ideas of John Winthrop." *New England Quarterly* 3 (1930): 235–50. Discusses Winthrop's philosophy of wealth and money-making.

McCrimmon, Barbara. "John Winthrop's Journal." *Manuscripts* 24 (1972): 87–96. Includes brief critiques of several journal entries.

Morgan, Edmund S. "John Winthrop's 'Modell of Christian Charity' in a Wider Context." *Huntington Library Quarterly* 50 (Spring 1987): 145–51. Argues that Winthrop's appeal for subjection to authority was a platitude and a common theme for shipboard communications.

Index

THE AUTHOR

Lee Schweninger received his Ph.D. from the University of North Carolina, Chapel Hill, and is currently assistant professor of English at the University of North Carolina, Wilmington. He has edited and introduced a collection of Puritan sermons, *Departing Glory: Eight Jeremiads by Increase Mather*, and has written several entries for the *Encyclopedia of American Literature*.